S. C. Gilman

The Story Of A Western Claim

A Tale Of How Two Boys Solved The Indian Question

S. C. Gilman

The Story Of A Western Claim
A Tale Of How Two Boys Solved The Indian Question

ISBN/EAN: 9783744708319

Printed in Europe, USA, Canada, Australia, Japan

Cover: Foto ©ninafisch / pixelio.de

More available books at **www.hansebooks.com**

By the Same Author.

THE FUTURE INDIAN

A BRIEF TREATISE ON THE INDIAN QUESTION

"Right to the point."—*Elaine Goodale.*

"The author writes discriminatingly."—*Indianapolis News.*

"Accept my thanks for your little book on the Indians. It is one of the most sensible articles I have seen on the subject, and well calculated to do good."—*Rev. John P. Williamson, twenty-six years a missionary worker among the Sioux Indians.*

THE STORY

OF A

WESTERN CLAIM:

A TALE OF HOW TWO BOYS SOLVED THE INDIAN QUESTION.

BY

S. C. GILMAN.

PHILADELPHIA:
PRINTED BY J. B. LIPPINCOTT COMPANY.
1893.

Copyright, 1893, by S. C. GILMAN.

CONTENTS.

CHAPTER I.
PAGE
A Peculiar Land Case 5

CHAPTER II.
The Poetry and Prose of Things 12

CHAPTER III.
Sowing the Seed 26

CHAPTER IV.
A New Philosopher comes to Light 40

CHAPTER V.
Strange Visitors 50

CHAPTER VI.
Smiles and Tears 69

CHAPTER VII.
New Life and New Hope 79

CHAPTER VIII.
Bright Days and Dark Ones 86

CHAPTER IX.
Light in Dark Places 93

CHAPTER X.
Reaping the Harvest 98

CHAPTER XI.
The Indian Boy's Manuscripts 105

CHAPTER XII.
An Old Question again Considered 128

CHAPTER XIII.
Conclusion 158

APPENDIX 175

THE STORY

OF A

WESTERN CLAIM.

CHAPTER I.

A PECULIAR LAND CASE.

"I'll tell ye, I don't believe the Lord ever intended any one fer to live in such a country as this. It ain't fit fer anything but coyotes to snarl 'round and hate theirselves in, an' I'm a-gettin' out of it as fast as I kin. Ye see, there's so much sand out here ye can't raise much of anything, an' what ye do raise ye can't sell, as there ain't any place fer to sell it. Ye simply break yer back all summer a-tryin' to make corn grow out'n the sand-heaps, an' then burn it all up durin' winter a-keepin' from freezin' to death. I heerd a feller say once that the Lord made all the rest of the earth first, an' then dumped the sand an' other leavin's down in here an' called it Nebrasky, and I guess he's about right. There's so much sand out here that the curiosest things have happened ye ever heerd of. Now, when Si Hopkins came into these parts he homesteaded a claim up near them jutes, 'longside Holt Creek. The soil is purty sandy there in some places, but Si got hold a claim that was all right, 'ceptin' forty acres off in one corner that had a sand-hill on it bigger'n a meetin'-house. Si, like a lot of other fellers what think they're goin' to come out here an' pick guv'ment bills off'n the plum-bush, soon soured on the country, and cleared out one day, a-sayin' he'd got enough of holdin' down a claim. Like a good many others, though, he came joggin' back afore the year was out, but he found a feller named Jim Blair had jumped his claim and took pre-emption papers on it. Si said he 'lowed he'd get the claim back some way, an' so, a-takin' up a claim next to the old one, that was all sand, he bided his time, as the poet says. Well, Jim went over to the county-seat one day durin' the winter, an' while he was there a blizzard came up, an' he couldn't get back ag'in fer three weeks because of the snow-drifts. When he did he found Si had taken possession of the claim, a-sayin' that a man didn't have no right fer to leave a pre-emption that long, an' he guess'd that he'd hold the claim down for a while now. Jim somewhat philosofically moved over to the sandy claim an' didn't make no kick to any one. In the course of time, Si went on to the reservation fer to steal cotton-wood logs, an' the first thing he knowed some Injuns rounded him up an' took him off to the agency; an' by the time he'd got things fixed up with the guv'ment, an' paid a fine fer trespassin', an' got 'round home, Jim was takin' life easy on the claim ag'in. Si had his ire up by this time, though, an' a-sayin' this fool business had got to end, he put a sod-shanty up on one edge of the land, an' there was two men a-holdin' down the same claim, an' both declarin' their right to it, the greatest case on record. The settlers got interested in the thing, an' the most of us rather inclined to'rds Si, as he'd got the claim in the first place. So Jim was made the victim of a surprise-party, which are very pop'lar in these parts, who took him out an' put a rope 'round his neck, an' run him up an' down underneath the limb of a cottonwood-tree several times, an' then he was let loose an' told he'd have to make tracks out of the neighborhood. But Jim only went back to his shanty, an' took down his shotgun, an' remarked he 'lowed he'd stay there for a while yet, an' he'd put air-holes through the first individual that middled in his business ag'in. People rather liked this kind of gameness,—it's very pop'lar in these parts,—an' so he wasn't bothered no more. Harvest came, an' Jim picked about forty bushels of corn, an' took it over to Mead's Ranch an' sold it fer fifty cents a bushel,—big thing in these parts, where corn usually sells fer a dollar a wagon-load, in exchange fer groceries,—an' then Si had him arrested fer sellin' stuff what was raised on his claim. Then Jim brought a suit fer damages ag'in Si fer alowin' cattle to run on his premises; an' this got the business into the courts finally, as to who owned that claim, anyhow, Si Hopkins or Jim Blair, an' I was on the jury that tried the case. That is, we tried to try it, an' when it come to a decision the jury split; six was for Si an' six was fer Jim, an' we hung out fer six days an' fer six nights, an' we couldn't git at no conclusion. At the end of the sixth night the jury had got purty well tuckered out, an' we'd all gone off to sleep, when a cyclone come along an' roused us all up, an' give us a fresh start. We had to 'journ to a house three miles away, though, as the court-house an' the county-seat wasn't no more. But the cyclone had blowed a little sense into us at the same time, an' we discovered the next day that we didn't have no business to be a-tryin' the case; it oughter have went to the land department at Valentine fer to be settled.

"But Jim, who had been down an' slept over-night on the claim (he wasn't a-goin' to let Si get any more p'ints agin' him), hunted up Si, an', takin' him off to one side, said, 'Now, the guv'ment's got to settle it, an' Lord knows when that'll be done. This thing's hung fire long enuff, an' I guess we'd better settle it ourselves. That claim is either your'n or mine. We can't both own it, an' we might as well fix the business up an' be done with it. I've made a few improvements on the claim; but you were there first, an' I calculate it wouldn't be no mor'n square fer me to pull up stakes an' get out, if ye'll only give me enough fer what's there to get away on.' So they dickered 'round fer awhile, and Jim finally agreed to take a hundred dollars, an' give up all rights to the claim. Si rustled up a hundred, and 'lowed he'd got a purty good bargain at that figure. The next day he drove over to the claim, an' say! there was the worst sight there you ever seen. The aforesaid cyclone had struck that sand-hill, the top of which had been ploughed over durin' the summer by Jim, an' flattened it out flatter'n a corn-cake; an' there was sand all over that claim two foot thick, an' there wasn't even room enough left fer to plant a melon-patch. Well, Si just stood there fer a minute or two, an' then he jumped astride his horse, an' took back to the county-seat like a wild man; but when he got there Jim Blair had vanished out of these parts, an' nobody has ever seen him since. But Si never got no sympathizin' words from me. After he'd got out of the country he'd oughter had better sense than to ever come back ag'in."

CHAPTER II.

THE POETRY AND PROSE OF THINGS.

PRAIRIETON was one of the first things primitive civilization created as it swept with a rush one day into a piece of unoccupied government territory that had been thrown open for settlement in a northern portion of Nebraska, and commenced the work of transforming a land of desolation into one of life and impulse. Albeit it was picturesque enough, with its little freshly-painted buildings, ornamented at intervals with sign-boards, bearing such unique inscriptions as "The Stag : Ale and Beer on Draught;" "Sam Kee, California Chinese Laundry;" and "Land and Loan Office;" yet one could hardly have desired it as a permanent residing-place. At least so thought George Eldredge and Paul

Morton, two young men from the East, as they walked up its one little street for the first time. Forty-eight hours before they had met each other in the passenger-station of a large Western railway in the city of Chicago, dropped into a conversation as travellers are apt to do, began to grow confidential as young travellers are more apt to do, discovered that both were out on the same mission; that both were going West to achieve greatness, fame, and fortune; that both had selected the same place wherein this was to occur; that both had tickets in their pockets for the same town; that both were waiting for the same train; and it is therefore unnecessary to state that a bond of friendship at once drew both together that years of acquaintance could not have made firmer or more perfect.

One does not generally get a favorable impression of a new frontier country, and it was so in the present case. Somehow, everything around looked uninviting,—so bleak and barren, and apparently so devoid of life, and offering no promise of any right away; so different from what the boys had pictured in their minds, that it would have taken very little to have induced them to board the next train going East.

As everybody wore wide-brimmed hats, and were clad in garments that spoke not of Eastern culture or Eastern styles, they felt painfully awkward and out of place with their black stiff hats, their white collars and neat cravats, and wandered away from the settlement for a little while.

Out on the prairie, a few rods to the north, was a "prairie schooner,"—that is to say, a canvas-covered wagon; and near it were some horses picketed. They went up to the outfit and found a hardy-looking man with his whole family, who had just abandoned a claim of government land north of the Niobrara River, and was starting back to the land of the rising sun to begin life over again.

"Left the East two years ago," he said to the boys. "Was a long time gettin' here, an' a long time gettin' out; but I'm started at last, ye see."

"Yes," said a second person, and a tired-faced but indignant-looking woman put her head out of the wagon, "and we sold one of the purtiest farms back East fer to git here, an' I always did say it was the durndest country I ever got in, an' I always did say it was your fault that we ever come out from the very beginning. John, you are an ole fool."

The man made no reply for a moment. Then he turned to the boys with an expression that spoke of both pain and resigned philosophical humor, and in a droll sort of way commenced to relate the remarkable story which graces the opening chapter of this narrative.

The boys were coming back into town towards noon when a small building, with the words "Weekly Herald Office" over the door met George's eyes. "I used to work in a printing-office back East," said George; "perhaps I might strike a job here."

Inside they found an old gentleman bent

over a case of type setting items for the next issue of the paper.

"He didn't want to hire anybody just then," he said, in response to George's inquiry; "but he intended to go East in the fall to remain all winter, and he should want somebody to run the office while he was away."

The boys started back to their hotel, and had nearly reached it when a stoutly-built, sharp-featured individual, with a smooth face and a sharp voice, came up and said,—

"Beg your pardon, young gentlemen; but I'm a land-agent. I'm doing a land and loan business out here. I'm posted on what land has been taken up and what has not. Now, I take it that you are looking for a claim. I locate people on claims. That's part of my business, and if you want a good A No. 1 claim that'll double in value in less than a year, I'm the fellow that'll put you on to one."

"Really," replied Paul, "we hardly know yet what we shall do. We had not thought over the matter of taking up a claim at all.

Perhaps we will find something to do in the town. We would prefer that to living on a claim."

"Pshaw," said the land-agent, "no matter what your business is, if you stay in this country you'll want a claim. Everybody out here holds down a claim. Every clerk in the town has one. The village attorney and the county judge both sleep on a claim at night. Now, I'll tell you what I'll do. Land's all taken up between here and the Niobrary; but there's some fine territory on the other side, and if you'd like to go I'll take you over there to-morrow, and show you some good claims."

The boys promised to see the agent in the afternoon, and, arriving at the hotel, they sat down and talked the matter over.

"Why not take up a claim," said George, "and stay on it altogether? I guess this country is not quite so sandy and bad as that settler would have us believe. It will only be a little while when it will all be built up, no doubt, and a claim of one hundred and sixty acres of government land that can now be had for almost nothing will be worth a small fortune. There will, probably, be some rough knocks,—a great deal of hardship and privation; but we are young and strong, and the reward that will come in the long run will be worth all our trouble. Suppose we do it."

As a result of this conversation, the two young men and the land-agent left Prairieton the next morning, behind a couple of spirited Indian ponies belonging to the latter, and were soon speeding over the prairie,—a vast expanse of land stretching away on either side like a troubled sea that had suddenly become motionless; for it was rolling prairie that looked level in many places, but really cut up into little swells and canyons that revealed themselves to the party as it went along.

Twenty-five miles north of Prairieton the party came to a great wide valley, at the bottom of which lay the Niobrara river. Descending into the valley, they crossed the stream over a wooden bridge that had just been completed.

"There's a quicksand bottom in that river in many places," said the agent. "Last spring one of them smart fellows from the East that can't be told anything attempted to drive through down by that willow-brush there. Him and the horses floundered for a minute as the treacherous bottom began to pull them down, and then it was all over with."

"Niobrara is its Indian term, is it not?" asked George.

"Yes," replied the agent; "or swiftly-flowing water; see how rapid the current is."

The whole neighborhood through which the party now began to pass was wild and desolate. All around them were dreary-looking little canyons, up whose sides stunted pine-trees were here and there growing. But occasionally they came to a better-timbered section, where huge cotton-wood-trees reared themselves to a height of fifty and sixty feet. Following the river for some distance, they turned into a canyon to the left, and then came a siege of climbing up-hill; not like going suddenly up a mountain-side, but a gradual ascent, with a good deal of winding around and twisting and turning, until suddenly the party found themselves on the edge of level land again, and looking back beheld the valley whose bottom-lands they had traced two hours before, apparently lying at their very feet.

As they went farther north the country became more desolate-looking than ever. There was nothing but land, land, everywhere,—a wilderness of land, with not a tree, not a shrub of any kind, growing upon it; simply land that stretched away to where a long range of hills reared themselves in curious shapes against a background of blue sky. No signs of life, either, unless it was when some timid, scared-looking rabbit revealed himself on a sand-knoll for a moment, and then flashed away over the prairie like mad; or when a flock of grouse arose right in front of the ponies, and with a loud whir-r-r soared into the sky.

As the ponies clattered along, the agent, for reasons best known to himself, kept up a stream of humor all the way, telling jokes and stories, and launching out into a song now and then not borrowed from the masters.

"See that streak of white over there," he said, finally, pointing to where a column of smoke was curling towards the sky; "that's where John Maynard, an old friend of mine, lives. He's a pretty good fellow, only he's got one bad fault,—he's always talking religion, and accounting for everything just like these Christians always do. Used to be a Methodist preacher back East, he told me once, but as he was getting pretty old, and didn't like the idea of being chucked off on to the superannuated list, he came out here several years ago, thinking he might get into something for himself. He brought a whole colony along with him, and built a town, and the first thing he put into it was a church, with revival meetings and all that sort of thing. He got himself appointed postmaster, and opened a grocery-store, and then he started a newspaper, and was booming things in great shape, when the news came that gold had been discovered in huge quantities somewhere up in the Black Hills, and everybody made a grand rush for that point, and the town was deserted in less than a week. Maynard went with them, too, for he'd mixed with the worldly enough by that time to have a little hankering after old Mammon himself. In two months the gold excitement played out, and so did the gold, and Maynard returned, but the colonists drifted away to other fields, and the town never became of any account again. One day he packed up his traps, and came over in here, took up a claim, built a sodhouse on it, and has remained ever since."

Just as dusk was coming on, the party drove up to the cabin where Maynard lived.

As they did so the door opened and an old man came out.

"Hello, Maynard," cried the land-agent, familiarly. "Over once more. Brought some young friends this time looking for land. Have to stay overnight, and show them the claims in the morning.

"Take the boys in," continued the land-agent, as the party got out of the wagon, "and I'll 'tend to the ponies."

"Well, boys," said Maynard, as he commenced preparing supper for the party, and after he had talked with the boys about their mission into that out-of-the-way region, "perhaps you'll succeed; but there's a good many trials and discouragements in a country like this. If you settle over here, though, I'll do all I can to help you."

The land-agent came in just as supper was ready, and though a plain, simple meal, it was relished by the travellers, whose appetites had been sharpened by the long day's journey.

The next morning the party, accompanied by Maynard, drove down along the bottom-lands of a stream separating the government land from the Sioux Reservation, lying to the north, and then coming up a slight elevation, the boys looked out upon a beautiful stretch of rolling prairie-land.

"Now, there," said the agent, with a sweep of his hand, "is one of the finest locations around these parts. It may seem pretty well out of the way now, but mind what I'm saying, this territory is all going to be settled up this summer. There's going to be another rush out here; it's started already, and you'll have plenty of company before fall."

The boys were well pleased with the land. They returned to Prairieton that day; applications were made for two filings, one a pre-emption in George's name, and the other a tree claim* in Paul's; the agent, of course, was paid for his services, and a week later the boys drove up to Maynard's door, ready to begin the life of claim-holders.

They were none too soon, for a few days

---

* The tree-claim law is now repealed.

afterwards they awoke to find a large tent on the level lands by the creek. A colony of land-seekers from the East had come over from Prairieton, and homesteading went on rapidly enough after that.

CHAPTER III.

SOWING THE SEED.

IN John Maynard the young claim-holders indeed found a valuable friend. In two weeks time, with his help, their prairie home was completed near the section-line dividing the pre-emption from the tree claim. The walls were made of prairie-sod cut into long strips two feet wide, and piled on each other to a height of eight or ten feet. Heavy cottonwood posts at each corner formed a good support for the roof, made of long poles placed against each other and covered with sod and a mass of dirt. With the clay, found in abundance along the bank of the creek, the walls were plastered over thoroughly inside, this giving the whole a neat appearance.

"The one great thing lacking," observed

Paul, "are board-floors in houses of this kind, but as there isn't a board or a saw-mill within eighty miles of here, I guess we'll have to make Mother Earth answer in our rough home for a while."

Yes, it was a rough home that few would have cared to live in, but, like many a rough thing in the world, it was the best home they ever had. For it was there the best lessons of their life were learned, where a rich experience was passed through that left them the possessors of a rich and noble manhood.

Another trip was made to Prairieton, where provisions and the household articles necessary for carrying on a "shantying" life were secured. A team and plough were next obtained from a farmer living south of the Niobrara, and the boys then entered into the work about their claims with great zeal. Sometimes they had many a hearty laugh at each other's expense, because of some woful blunder that Maynard would show them they had committed, but the work was done after a rude fashion, and by the first of May all the ground they intended to cultivate was ploughed and put to seed,—two large fields, one planted to corn and the other sown to wheat, and a smaller one planted with potatoes. Close to the cabin a " garden patch" was started, "from which," exclaimed Paul, one day, " we'll get enough onions and cucumbers and lettuce and radishes to feed a regiment of soldiers, let alone two young exiles far from the madding crowd of the East."

The most important part of their work being over, a fishing-expedition was decided upon. Just across the river, not a mile to the north, lay the Sioux Reservation, and back of the hills paralleling the river flowed a stream, Maynard said, that swarmed with the finny tribe. Supplied with lines and bait, the boys, accompanied by the old settler, left at an early hour one morning, and wading the river where it lay shallow on a bed of gravel, they climbed over the sandy hills, picking up, as they went along, pieces of petrified wood and curiously-shaped stones.

At the top of a high peak, which the party ascended, they looked towards the north, and beheld a vast rolling plain stretched out before them like a deserted world.

"What a contrast," exclaimed George, "between this place and Chicago! and yet how short the time may be when this will be changed; and even now, perhaps, we are looking upon a spot where a great city will some day be built, and these plains around it teem with life and industry. And who knows what wealth may lie beneath our very feet,—gold, it may be,—stored away and only waiting for man to come and search it out." As he spoke, Maynard gave a quick start, which was unobserved, and the boy continued, "But why wait for the white race alone to come and do all this? This is not our land; this land belongs to the Indians. In one sense we might say that it does not, but in another that it does. If the Indians show no disposition to develop it, and let it remain an unbroken wilderness, let us assume that it ought to pass into the ownership of another race that will. For one race of people to lay claim to vast tracts of land, upon which man may dwell, and the genius which God has given him may find expression; for a small race to set up an ownership to such estates, and then simply occupy the same as little wandering nomadic tribes, it seems, indeed, the worst kind of folly; but if God made it possible for the Indians to become civilized and intelligent like ourselves, does it not follow that He placed them upon this land upon which they might so live and thrive? And if, perchance, they have wandered away from the manhood in which they were first created, and have become as we now find them, and if we presume to be the means, as children yet dwelling in the light and grace of God, by which these Indians may be brought back again, must we not concede that the land is theirs; and teaching them to become like ourselves,—like the God in whose image all men were first created,—leave to them the portion God intended should be theirs?"

"But again," said Paul, "may it not be that the Indian's faith and manner of worship are acceptable to God, for are they not sincerely rendered? And may it not be that God created him to be a child of nature, happy in his own way of living?"

"Nay," interposed Maynard. "I cannot look at it in that light. All men were intended to reach the highest plane of manhood, and to have but one true faith,—the faith of light and reason. Jesus, the Son of God, represented both of these. In Him were personified the highest and best qualities of manhood, and He it is whom all men should look up to and imitate. Out of a belief in God and the Saviour there has come into the world our Christian civilization, embodying the best form of society that has yet existed among men. To all who enjoy its blessings there comes the obligation of carrying the same to all who are without it; and this we should not fail to do, as George has said, in the case of the Indians."

"It often depends upon the point from which you view things," replied Paul. "Now, suppose an Indian would come and hold up the mirror before us, wherein we would behold our own civilization as others see it,—men divided into classes and as far from each other socially as the East is from the West. Men arrayed against each other in the business and industrial life,—the capitalist and laborer formed into societies to protect themselves against each other. Men with everything at their command, with untold wealth, and everything the heart may desire, and by their very side men struggling in want and no one to offer the hand of sympathy and aid. In the slums of our great cities,—creatures of civilization,—men sunk to the lowest depths of degradation, who debauch themselves and prey upon their fellow-men, and who are several degrees lower than the meanest Indian that ever lived. And amidst it all the Church, the heart of civilized life, doing so little to counteract the evils around it? What would you say to all this?"

"Your last sentence," said Maynard, with a smile, "would imply that the Church was not responsible for these evils, and, if she only did more than she does, these evils might be done away with. The fact is, Paul, society is what its individuals are. The individual is what the heart is. These evils that afflict society grow out of the heart and nature of the individual man, and society then will be purified and made more perfect, these evils diminished, and the Church more firmly established just as men's hearts become touched, and men are convinced of what constitutes Right in the world; and so I would ask Mr. Indian to hold the mirror up again, and I would show him all that is pure and good and highest in civilization,—the Christian part of it,—and then I would ask him why he should reject the one because the other existed. And while it is a sad thought that much of this evil might not now exist, had the Church been more active, is that any reason why Christianity and the Church should be deserted, and the life she offers should not be accepted? If you were one of a crew, manning a life-boat on a storm-tossed sea, Paul, and all around you were human beings struggling in the waves, but the crew were lying back on their oars and doing nothing to rescue them, would you forsake the boat, and leap out into the waves to perish with those already going down, or, still retaining faith in your mission, would attempt to continue the work, single-handed and alone? Would it not be better to remain on board, rouse the whole crew to a sense of their duty, and save all whom you could?"

Threading their way down into a little canyon, the party came out on the banks of a stream that sparkled beneath the sun like a band of silver.

"Here's where we get fish that is fish,"

said Maynard, pausing beneath a great cottonwood that shaded part of the stream, and baiting his hook, cast it over towards the water. The hook had barely touched the surface, when it made a dive underneath, and a second later a big bass lay flopping on the bank.

"My! That was done quick," exclaimed George, whose line was hardly in shape yet.

"Oh, these Western fish are no tenderfeet," chuckled the old sportsman, as he baited the hook, threw it over again, and then, to the boys' amazement, hauled in another bass larger than the first; "they don't nibble around an hour or two, and then go shooting off upstream as though they had just thought of something there they wanted. They bite on the go-in, and they're pretty hungry just now."

The boys were not as successful as Maynard, but once in a while they both pulled out a young flopper from his watery retreat. The party moved along the banks of the stream for some distance, and at noon, coming to a little grove of cottonwoods, they built a fire in its shade, eating roasted fish with the lunch they had brought along. They then resumed their tramp through the brush along the creek, and the day wore away before they knew it.

Suddenly a low, deep rumble broke the stillness, causing them to start and look around.

"Was there ever a fishing-trip without a rain-storm?" cried Paul.

"Not when you go poaching on the reservation,—land that belongs to the Indians," shouted Maynard.

"Never thought about that," exclaimed George; "serves us right, I say."

Over in the northwest the sky was growing densely black, thick clouds rolling up from the horizon, and flashing out sheets of fire every second or two.

"As to the rights or wrongs of this expedition," cried Maynard, "that's a subject for future discussion. The thing now to do is to —*git*. Follow me."

Away they dashed, with Maynard in the lead, until they reached a point where the bank shelved directly down to the edge of the creek, a mass of spreading willows growing at the top, forming a natural covering to the ground below.

"We'll huddle up here," said Maynard, "and I guess we can keep out of the worst part of the storm."

Just as he spoke, there was a crash, followed by a series of crashes, as though the heavens had suddenly become filled with artillery-guns, and all commenced going off at once. There is something new and refreshing about a thunder-storm on the prairie. The thunder starts up a regular continuous roar, and peals follow one right after another, the lightning spitting sharply and spitefully, and the noise and racket and fire seem to get down on to the earth in a heap.

That was the kind of a storm George and Paul encountered for the first time, and it is hardly necessary to say they did not like it.

When the party ventured from their retreat the ground was soaked and the prairie grass dripping with water.

When they reached home Maynard concluded not to stay with the boys overnight, and after supper started away in the darkness. As he walked along he commenced talking to himself, as people are very apt to do when anything of great importance weighs down upon the mind.

"It's been some time," he said, "since I left the Hills, and settled down here to find freedom from the madness that such a life brings. I thought it was all through with, but that remark of George's has brought the old fever back again. There's gold in those hills across the river. I've often thought it, and now I know it. Old Maynard, you are not of much account, and it's pretty late in life, that's sure, for an old stick like yourself to begin hammering in the earth again for wealth; but there's the boys,—they've come, and they'll need it, and if I can only help somebody,—

and especially two such lads as they,—it will be all that I shall ask."

Then he paused and reflected a moment, and then continued,—

"Maybe it's madness to think so; the wild dream of an old man. Perhaps it is the unconquerable impulse that is forever coming upon one to dig—dig—dig, who once gets this gold-mining fever into his system. But something has always seemed to tell me there is gold in those hills, and if there is I'll find it. Why should I tell the boys of my purpose? If I fail, they will have been saved the disappointment that would follow, and, besides, it were better they should go ahead with the work they have undertaken."

CHAPTER IV.

A NEW PHILOSOPHER COMES TO LIGHT.

IN the morning, when the boys awoke, they found the rain coming down in torrents. The weather due the month before was now at hand, and although it meant enforced confinement for the boys for a few days, they did not murmur, but, like wise old farmers, rejoiced over the prospect of a good start for the crops. In the forenoon George opened an iron-bound trunk that he had brought from the East, and down in the bottom, packed snugly away, was a collection of books, papers, and magazines,—a regular mine of literature that set Paul's eyes to sparkling. As George was about to take a book out and hand it to Paul, the latter, who was stooping over his shoulder, exclaimed,—

"What's that roll of manuscripts there with a string around it?"

A flush spread over George's face. He looked quite surprised for a moment, and then said, with a weak attempt at a smile,—"Oh, that's some scribbling of my own. I once thought I was an author. Behold the result."

And as he spoke he held up the roll by the string before Paul, who, instead of bursting into a laugh, said, seriously enough,—

"Well, what are you looking so queer about? There is nothing in the calling of an author to be ashamed of, is there?"

"No," replied George, brightening up, "but there's nothing worse than a man who thinks he is an author and isn't, who tries to be an author and fails."

"What's your line?" said Paul, running his hands down into his pockets and looking very grave,—"poetry or prose?"

"Mostly prose," answered George; "but I have dashed off a few poetical lines, too; would you like to hear some of them?"

"By all means," was the reply.

Untying his manuscripts, George ran his fingers through the leaves, until he came to a page, where he stopped.

"Now, here's a simple little piece," he said, "that endeavors to show what constitutes true greatness in this world.

"TRUE GREATNESS.

"In the ancient days of ballad rhyme,
 When lords and barons held full sway,
 And nightly held their revels, and quaffed their ruddy
   wine,
 The world lived for conquest and for fray.
And the grandest man of all,
 The greatest one was he,—
The knight who marched into the banquet hall,
 All laden down with war trophy.

"But now, when Light and Truth shine brighter than the sun,
 Instead of vulture dark,
The gentle dove of peace has come
 And nestles in man's heart;
And the greatest one that I can find,
 The grandest I can know,
Is he whose love goes out to all mankind,
 Who does not want a foe."

"Great!" exclaimed Paul. "Give us another."

It is pleasant to record that a friendly eye never sees the faults or weak points in a thing of one's construction, however glaring they may appear to others.

"In the struggle of life," said George, "where 'man's inhumanity to man makes countless thousands mourn,' there is many a soul who may be cheered by such lines as these:

"TO THE DISCOURAGED FRIEND.

" Oh, tired friend, dear tired friend,
　Half wishing all were at an end,—
　Tired of the bitter, ceaseless strife,
　Of blighted hopes and a saddened life,
　Do not despair, but toil along
　And lighten thy burden with a song;
　For trial is often but the test
　That wins for one the sweetest rest.
　When mortal man has turned to clay;
　When proud and meek have gone their way;
　When weak and strong, and bond and free
　Are gathered down at death's dark sea,
　Then he whose faith's been greatest tried
　Shall gain the best and brightest side."

"In human life," said George, laying the papers down, "men plan and build as though it were eternal, forgetting that death is in the world, and even as we build the silent reaper comes along and takes us away, and all that we have constructed soon passes into decay. How much better it is, then, to look beyond this life, and build for that eternity which awaits us beyond the grave! Human life has its purposes, and the chief end of man is to glorify God. In doing this, then, and in practising the heavenly virtues in mortal life, we shall be called to have a part in that higher immortal existence which knows no ending, where death and decay never come. The Good Book tells us," he continued, "that the 'trying of your faith worketh patience,' and in patience lies the key to true happiness in human life. And so, as this little poem also implies, while justice should exist in the world, and all deserving men should have equal privileges, yet if justice is not granted a man, and all that he has be taken from him, if he has the faith to believe that should it not be so in this life, yet all wrongs shall be righted, he will obtain first of all the sweetest of virtues,—patience,—and with faith as his strength and with patience as his weapon he will gain the victory over the whole world, no matter how much of trial may be poured into his life. All this applies equally as well to the ambitious ones. Ambition has its place in the world when it seeks to better the world and human kind; but if the most deserving one, with nothing but the highest of ideals and the best of purposes, goes forth into life with bright expectations, and finds instead failure, and never receives the recognition which should be his, even becoming doomed to a condition where he must bear

> 'the whips and scorns of time,
> The oppressor's wrong, the proud man's contumely,
> *   *   *   *   *   *
> The insolence of office, and the spurns
> That patient merit of the unworthy takes,'

"he may show himself the greatest of heroes by meeting it all with unbroken patience and unfaltering faith in the belief that things will yet turn out for the best.

"Why this brief philosophical dissertation on human life?" continued George, with a smile. "Well, you see, I grew up in a large community in the East, and was ambitious. When a boy I fixed certain ideals deep in my mind, to which I proposed to attain when I should reach manhood. After the school-days I went to work in a large publishing-house in the city where I lived, taking an inferior position at first, hoping to rise to an important place in the house, to be among the literary force, and to be able to bring my writings before the public. But the prospect of promotion was poor, indeed. I never had the pluck to submit any of my manuscript for publication, or even tell any one about the same, fearing they would be rejected and of the ridicule that would then surely follow from my associates in the office. To make matters worse, there were frequent 'lay-offs,' owing to the dull seasons in our business, times when there is nothing to do and weeks of enforced idleness come along. So, what with 'dull seasons' and 'crushed ambition,' I became completely discouraged, and instead of patiently

'toiling along,
Lightening my burden with a song,'

I cleared out one day, telling my folks they would never see me again until I could come back my own master and my dreams realized; all of which," concluded the speaker, with a grim smile, "suggests the thought that if my poem, accompanied by these extended remarks, should go out to the world, I would, no doubt, be accused of insincerity by the critical reader, of not setting the exemplary example of practising what I preach."

"I think," said Paul, as George finished speaking, " that the world is pretty much the same wherever one goes. And from the general indication of things" (casting his eyes significantly around at their rough surroundings), "before we get through with our life out here we shall have a chance to live up to the spirit of your poem, and you will have a splendid opportunity of showing yourself neither insincere nor a hypocrite."

So the days, damp and cheerless enough on the outside, were made profitable within by much of reading and rough philosophizing, until one morning Paul was awakened by a vigorous shaking, and George's voice ringing in his ears,—

"Hurrah, Paul, our old friend's come back once more! get up and give him a welcome."

"Who's here? What old friend?" exclaimed Paul, as he raised up in bed.

"Why, the sun, of course; we are going to have some decent weather for a change."

It had cleared up in the early part of the night, and, looking to the east, the boys beheld through their little window the sun just above the horizon, away to the end of miles of prairie land, swinging slowly upward in a flood of crimson.

After one has been shut up six days in a

sod-shanty, one feels like going into ecstasies at a sight like this.

A walk about the claim that morning showed the corn and wheat just peeping above the ground in little green blades, and as the boys went back to their cabin Paul commenced whistling back at a lot of meadow-larks that had settled down all around, and commenced pouring out a chorus of mellow pipings. Then he stopped and exclaimed,—

"I say, George, things are looking bright now."

"That's what they are," was the reply.

CHAPTER V.

STRANGE VISITORS.

ONE early morning, when George stepped from the door of the cabin, an exclamation of surprise burst from his lips. An Indian village had sprung up during the night as if by magic, and all around were Indian " teepees," twenty-five or thirty in number. The tents or "teepees" were closed tightly at the entrance, and not a sound of any kind could be heard from within to indicate the presence of life.

The boys at once became alarmed over the presence of their strange visitors, and George, who had found it possible to plead in behalf of the Indian, now found it another matter to meet him face to face. Perhaps all that he needed was a little more moral courage.

A hasty departure for Maynard's place was

being discussed when that individual himself came in, laughed at the boys' fears, and said,—

"Haven't become acquainted with those people yet, have you? Was a time when a person'd felt like having business elsewhere if he'd woke up some morning and found a swarm out there like that. But there's no danger nowadays. The Indians are all 'good Indians,'—just now, anyhow,—and they're about the only neighbors a person has in these quarters."

The boys thereupon commenced getting breakfast, and Maynard showed them how to cook a mess of meal-cakes, which were nothing else than old-fashioned New England "johnny-cakes," baked, however, no larger than ordinary biscuits. These were placed in a pan on the centre of the table, making a great steaming heap, and with a few slices of bacon, some cold cooked corn, and a mug of sparkling water, made up the morning meal.

The settlers had just taken their seats at the table when a deep guttural "Ugh!" caused them to start and look towards the door. A Sioux Indian stood in the door-way. The form from the shoulders down was shrouded in a dirty canvas blanket, from the bottom folds of which the feet, encased in moccasons, protruded; while an old straw hat, resting squarely and well down on a head of thick, mane-like hair, completed the make-up. His countenance, dark, copper-colored, wore a stolid expression, and round, bead-like eyes met the settlers' gaze, as they looked upon the strange-looking new-comer.

His whole appearance was anything but prepossessing, but, coming forward, he said,—

"How do? Me Red Wing. Me big chief. Me no bad Indian. White man got good big teepee. When you come? Ugh!"

"Hello! old fellow," replied Maynard, as he stepped to the Indian and slapped him vigorously on the back. "How are you, anyhow?"

A smile spread over the broad, dark face.

"Ugh! Me know you. You old Dog Face. Ugh! How do?"

A burst of laughter greeted this sally, and Red Wing extended his hand from the folds of his blanket, which the three shook heartily.

When the Indian was about to leave the room, George handed him a couple of hot buttered cakes, and the poor fellow devoured them greedily as he went away from the cabin.

"Now you have done it," said Maynard.

"What do you mean?" asked George.

"Just wait a minute and you'll see," was the reply.

The settlers had hardly finished their breakfast, when a babel of voices outside of the cabin led George to the door, where he was greeted by an assemblage of squaws,— with their "pappooses" slung across their backs in a shawl,—all of whom commenced imploring in one voice for the cakes, and, as there was no other alternative, the pan was brought out and soon deprived of its contents.

By ten o'clock the whole Indian village was astir. Squaws flitted here and there, some bringing water, others building fires in front of the "teepees," while the aboriginal lords sat around in various attitudes, or wandered out over the prairie with their ponies.

"These 'teepees,'" said Maynard to the boys, as the three examined the odd-looking structures, "are not made like the ones they used to have. Buffalo-skins were once used for coverings The skins were sewed together with sinews, and stretched on long poles, but the buffalo are all gone now, and the Indians have to use this canvas, which is furnished by the government."

In front of each structure large stakes were driven into the ground, in such manner as to form a support for a large iron pot or kettle, under which a hot fire was kindled.

The settlers learned that the Indians were from one of the agencies in Dakota, and were on their way to a neighboring reservation, where some Indian sports were to be held.

Some of the male Indians were communicative, but the majority appeared sullen and disposed to hold aloof from the settlers.

Indians are great traders, however, and one, attracted by a bright chain which adorned Paul's vest, offered to exchange a pair of beaded moccasons for the same. The chain was a gift from a friend in the East, and Paul could only refuse to part with it. The Indian was so determined to make a trade, that finally Paul produced a couple of brass rings from his pocket, which caught the Indian's eye at once, and for which he parted with the moccasons, highly elated over the bargain.

The Indians remained several days, and the young settlers learned much of their life and customs. On the day before their departure it was announced that an Omaha dance would be given in the evening, and settlers came in from all over the region to witness the curious affair. Some anonymous writer has thus described this dance:

"The Sioux have many dances, but the

Omaha dance is the most popular of all. It carries the old man back to his days of murder, horse-stealing, and hair-breadth escapes, and keeps the young buck* an Indian in the truest sense of the name. The great drum is always with the Omaha. Its time is the monotonous tom, tom, tom, tom, with an occasional 'hi-a, hi-a, hi, hi, hi,' ending with a great bang and a chorus of yells. The dancers, all men and boys, are rigged up for the occasion in most gorgeous array and grotesque style. Some wear war-bonnets made of eagle-feathers that reach from their heads to their heels. Others wear horses' tails instead of bustles. The head-gearing is from a buffalo-head down to a bird's head. Many wear simply a head-cloth, while their bodies are painted in all imaginable shapes and of all shades. Their faces are always painted with either vermil-

---

* An Indian is invariably referred to as a "buck" by the people of the frontier.

ion, chrome-yellow, green, or ultra-marine blue, alone or in combination with an occasional use of lamp-black. Sleigh-bells and jingling ornaments, the pipe and the eagle feather, complete the arrangements of the company, which circles into a great ring. The proceedings begin. If on a cold day or night, a fire is built in the centre, adding cheerfulness to the occasion. The drum, presided over by half a dozen Indians, is beating the tom, tom, tom in about common time; a few rise up and begin to go through the dance, followed by the others, until the whole circle stamp the ground in a very vigorous manner. A rest comes. Suddenly a dancer comes from the circle with a bow or gun in hand. He stalks about, dodging here and there. In a moment another Indian, representing another tribe, comes similarly prepared. Each goes through a motion of some kind, either creeping or running; advancing or retreating. The combat finally occurs and the Sioux has killed his enemy.

Then the successful actor makes a speech to the assembled dancers, reviewing his brave acts in detail. Sometimes a horseman goes through an exploit, falling gracefully from his horse, as if dead, when some friendly Indian passes by and nourishes him to life. But the most prevalent scene is that of horror and treachery, and they glory in them and are glorified by such traits. Then more dancing is indulged in, and between each rest some scene is acted, or speech made reciting deeds of the past. A feast of tender dog is always in order. The dance 'teepees' or lodges afford considerable room, but where the Indians are permanently located more commodious quarters are provided."

Such were the scenes enacted before a large assemblage of settlers on this occasion. The dance was not produced on as grand a scale as it would have been at an agency, or by a larger band of Indians. Several Indians surrounded a drum, and kept up a steady, dull thumping, keeping time with their voices, while from the small circle of participants a half-naked figure would leap out into the centre every few moments and go through the most grotesque movements imaginable.

As the dance reached its height, George turned to a settler standing beside him, and said,—

"Well, is it any wonder that the Indians do not make much progress in the Christian civilization when they are allowed to revel in the very things that are directly opposed to it? Living in teepees, wandering from one nook to another, indulging in feasts, dances, and orgies,—this is hardly conducive to Christianity. We had better have had nothing to do with the Indians at all, if we simply furnish them the means to continue the existence in which we find them, and make no effort to lift them up to anything higher. But, surely, there is a better class than the one represented here. I suppose now at the agencies we would find a more advanced element,—the ones who have been brought under the influence of missions and the schools which the government has established."

"Oh, they talk about a better element,— progressive Indians they call them," was the reply, "but I tell you they are few and far between. Fact of the matter is, there ain't any. There ain't any good Indians, but a dead——"

"But," interrupted George, "what of the educated ones,—the young Indians who are placed in the schools I have mentioned?"

"Worst ones in the whole lot," was the answer. "If you want to put the finishing touches on the treacherous nature which an Indian possesses, just endow him with a little intelligence, and give him a knowledge of the white man and his ways, and then he can think and lay his devilish plans better than he could before, and is more dangerous than ever."

"But, surely," George remonstrated, "they are not *all* treacherous. Have you never seen any good instance among them?"

"No," answered the settler. "Been forty

years on the frontier, and never seen but one kind of Indian. An Indian is an Indian, and you can't make anything else out of him. He's too lazy to be otherwise. Why, I've seen young fellows come back from the schools in the East, where they had probably been for six or eight years,—coming back and looking as spruce as could be,—but in less than three months they would have their blankets on again; long-haired, dirty, and lazy-looking as ever, and you couldn't any more get a word of English out of them than you could that post yonder. As I was remarking before, the only good Indian is a dead——"

"There are always two sides to every question," said George; "perhaps we could find an explanation for this should we care to look for it."

"There may be two sides to the Indian question," remarked another settler, who had been listening to the conversation, "but I never could see but one. I have about as much love for an Indian as I have for a coyote. Wait until you have one of them get after your scalp, young fellow, and you'll think the same way. My solution of the question would be to gather all the red devils into a bunch and then put a can of dynamite underneath them, and blow the whole business into the kingdom come, and you can depend upon it the question would be effectually solved then."

"I'll tell you how it is," said a third Solon. "An Indian is just like a buffalo. He wants room. When you close in on him he disappears,—just like the buffalo. Fifty years from now there won't be an Indian; he'll be as completely exterminated as the wild bison that used to roam these prairies."

"Let's see," said George. "I understand there are about two hundred and fifty thousand Indians still living. Of these twenty-five thousand are Sioux. I cannot see how our own neighbors are going to all disappear in so short a time, let alone the rest, unless we adopt the humane policy that has been suggested, and apply the use of dynamite."

"Well, I'll tell you, gentlemen," said an intelligent-looking man who had been standing quietly by. "The best way to settle this Indian problem is to adapt the Indian to that which is best suited to his nature, that which he most prefers. The leopard cannot change its spots. The lion cannot become a lamb. The Indian can never become a civilian and a man of peace. He cannot and never has been able to endure the restraints of civilization, any more than the eagle has been able to survive the confinement of the tamer's cell. He loves the wild, free part of human existence, and to him the highest type of manhood is that which shines out in the warrior. With this warlike disposition, with all the elements in his nature that make the true soldier, it seems to me the government could do no better than to enlist him in the service of the army. Wherever this has been done, whenever he has been employed as a scout, he has proven of incalculable value, especially on account of his knowledge of the country, and his powers of endurance which such a life calls for. Whenever engaged to perform police duties among his own people, the government has never found a more faithful servant, and one more loyal in time of serious trouble. And, best of all, if the Indians were all enlisted in the regular service, they would at last be given something to do; they would at last learn to become more self-sustaining, and cease to be the helpless dependents upon the government they have always been." *

The Omaha dance was over. The settlers had gone away. The Indians had retired to their lodges, and all outside was hushed and quiet. For some reason George could not sleep, and turned restless about in bed. Presently he arose and dressed, and went

---

* See "Indians as Soldiers," Appendix.

out in front of his cabin. It was a brilliant moonlight night. The sky above, never appearing more vast and expansive than in a level prairie region, was now a perfect mass of stars,—thousands upon thousands, sparkling and glittering,—looking like a huge canopy beset with massive diamonds. As George looked up at the magnificent spectacle, and out over the prairie now bathed in a flood of golden light, he exclaimed,—

"It must be on such a night as this that departed spirits like to visit the earth, if they ever come back at all. When I die, if my soul is permitted to return to earth, I shall select such a night for my ghostly perambulations."

"Do you think you would really care about coming back?" said a voice, so suddenly and unexpectedly that it startled George half out of his senses, and for an instant he thought some ghostly visitor had indeed come upon him.

Turning, he beheld a Sioux, a young man not much older than himself.

"I beg your pardon," said the Indian, "for taking you so unawares, but the question seemed so timely, I could not help asking it."

An Indian, standing before him in the garb of the half-civilized members of his race, nearly as wild-looking and uncouth as the ones who had been dancing the weird Omaha dance, yet addressing him in English as politely as he had ever heard it spoken.

George simply stared at the boy in amazement and made no reply. "Well," he thought, "the settlers are right, for here is a living illustration of what they have said."

"You are surprised," continued the speaker, "but you will not be, perhaps, after you have heard my story. Ever since we have been in camp here I have felt that I must come to you and speak of my life,—so strange, so different than your own,—a life for which the world seems to care very little, and yet a human life that once possessed all the heart-longings and ambition that come to the enlightened human soul. But as to the things of which

I would speak, I cannot talk to-night. They who wait for me in my lodge do not know what I have done, and I must hasten back to them. Perhaps I will come again, but if I do not, you will find written down here all that I would say to you, all that I would have you hear."

Pausing, the Indian drew from beneath the breast of his shirt a roll of manuscripts, and handing them to George, darted away and became lost in the shadows that hung about the group of lodges a short distance away.

"Was it not a dream?" said George the next morning, when he arose.

No; there was the roll of manuscripts the Indian boy had given him, lying upon the table.

He picked the papers up and turned them over in his hands for a moment.

"It contains the story of his life, which I am to read. But he said he might return to me again. Why not wait until then? I should prefer to talk with him, to hear the story from his own lips. He's a deserving fellow, I am quite sure, and there is something in him. Let me see. I will put the papers in the trunk with my own manuscripts, though, where I can find them again."

"Pshaw!" he exclaimed, a little later, "what in the world is the use of that boy wasting his young life among these people? I will hunt him out to-day and persuade him to leave them, to remain here with me, and whatever his story may be, or whatever else he would have me to know, here I will learn all, and here he and I may learn to understand each other, and learn to work together."

He went to the door and looked out.

The lodges were gone.

The Indians had stolen away early in the morning while he was still soundly sleeping.

CHAPTER VI.

SMILES AND TEARS.

THREE months had wrought a great change in the country, at first a prairie wilderness. A day seldom passed that did not bring a new party of land-seekers, and there was scarcely a claim in the whole region not settled upon now. Some of the settlers had relinquished their claims for a fair consideration and gone farther West, and once or twice Paul and George had offers made to them of a like character.

The boys were eating dinner, one day, when a stranger drove up to the door and dismounted. He had just come from Iowa, he said, and was looking for a piece of land. He wanted some improved territory, and had been looking the boys' claims over a day or two before. He was pleased with their appearance, and complimented the boys as successful young farmers. Then he said,—

"To come to the point, and without any unnecessary parleying, I will give you eight hundred dollars for the two relinquishments, which will be four hundred dollars apiece. I am satisfied the land is worth that much, and I want to do what should be my part in an honorable business transaction."

Eight hundred dollars,—four hundred apiece! Why, they hadn't seen a dollar for a month. The stranger's proposition almost took their breath away.

Would they sell? George was almost in the act of jumping to his feet and telling the stranger to take the land, house, old clothes, and everything about the place; and even Paul pinched himself to see if he had fallen off to sleep, and the whole thing was a dream. But, dreaming or not, he was awake to second thought in another moment. Eight hundred dollars was a good sum of money for two boys who had never owned a hundred. But what did it represent in this case? The value of their claims,—three hundred and twenty acres of land,—a little over two dollars an acre. Two dollars and a half for a whole acre of rich, productive land, that in another year might be worth twenty at least. No, it would never do. George, too, was beginning to show signs of reflection, and when Paul spoke it was to express the sentiment of both.

"Well, your offer may be a good one; but, after all, it seems a small amount for so much land. Our claims are among the best around here, and a great deal has been sacrificed by us,—an awful amount of labor done here this summer. We'd like to sell, if we could get a fair offer; but if we cannot, we will wait until land is worth something around, and we can get enough for all our trouble. We ought to have at least twelve hundred dollars. A great many settlers value one claim alone at that amount."

The stranger thought the price too high; couldn't think of paying so much. He had already had several chances to buy land at less terms than those he offered the boys; but he liked their location, and was willing to pay a little more. However, he would give them nine hundred dollars if they would close the bargain at once.

The boys were silent for a few moments. Nine hundred dollars; that was small enough, and yet with it a great deal could be done. Something more congenial to their taste than that of farming could be gone into, and the vision of a newspaper-office, with himself buried in a mass of manuscripts and newspapers, came before George,—the realization of a dream he had had in his mind since coming West. But, then, this was all too sudden, anyhow. There were many things to be settled, and they ought by all means to be given a little more time for a decision.

Finally, the stranger agreed to wait a couple of days, and then departed. He had hardly disappeared beyond the swell of land that lay a few miles away, when the boys began to regret they had not accepted his offer. Their lonely life, fraught with toil and privation, had often put their pluck to the test; and now, just at a time when they were almost penniless, and passing through a siege anything but pleasant, a chance to escape from it all had come, and they had thrown it away, perhaps.

Another day passed, and still another, and when finally a whole week went by and the stranger failed to appear, the boys concluded that he had bought land elsewhere, and gave up looking for him.

A long dry spell had come. The "drought," something that always breaks in upon a new agricultural region just at the most inopportune time, had arrived. "Heat-winds" were blowing over the prairie. The crops were burning up. Everything seemed going to destruction. It was hot, hot, insufferably hot. The young claim-holders had never seen anything like it before, and, worst of all, there was no getting away from it,—no grove, no trees, beneath the shade of which relief might be found. Cabins afforded but little protection. Inside, they were like sweat-boxes. Outside, one could sprawl out close to the wall, which threw a dark line over the ground, changing one's position as the sun mounted higher, and the shadow grew smaller until it disappeared, and then appeared again on the other side of the house.

"We shall have a storm sure to-night," the boys had said at first, when night after night the sky would be lit up with great flashes of lightning, soon learning that that was no indication; it was merely "heat-lightning," that plays around the horizon every evening nearly in the prairie country in summer-time.

But late one afternoon, when the claim-holders were longing for the sun to go down, a breath of cool air swept in from the northwest; then a few clouds appeared, very soon the distant rumbling of thunder was heard, and in a few moments more the whole western sky was dark with heavy clouds.

"Hurrah!" cried Paul, "we're going to have rain at last."

But wait a moment, Paul. A storm is coming, yet not of the kind suited to your desire.

The sky is now filled with rolling, angry clouds, the wind is blowing a perfect gale, and, as the boys look towards the west, suddenly they behold a funnel-like cloud, whirling around and around, coming towards them and striking the earth apparently in long leaps.

In another instant they knew what it all meant,—a cyclone was sweeping down upon them. Early in the spring, following Maynard's advice, they had made a large cave-cellar near the cabin in case of a destructive storm; ever since it had been the butt for constant jokes, but now a cyclone had really come, and it was to be a refuge for their lives.

Running to the cave, they entered it and

closed the opening just as the curious-looking cloud swept over the spot. Intrenched as they were in their snug retreat, they could not tell what destruction was being done outside; they only heard the noise of the storm which came to them in muffled sounds, and when these ceased they ventured out. But what a scene met their eyes!

Their sod-house was gone. Their little prairie home had been completely swept away, and all around it seemed as though nothing but blank ruin existed. A shower of great hailstones had beat furiously down during the progress of the storm, and all over the fields corn and wheat lay flattened on the ground, in some places completely broken from the stalk.

The most of us can laugh down the failures and misfortunes of life; such experiences often give us new zeal and a firmer determination to yet live and conquer, but when they first come the bravest heart will give way for a moment. As the two boys beheld all this destruction,—the ending that had come to weeks of toil and hardship,—it was too much. They simply stood there for a while, and—who would not have done the same?—tears are by no means an indication of weakness.

"Well," said Maynard, who had hurried over to the boys' claims, "there's no use crying over spilt milk, and I can't see as there's any use mourning over a spilt claim. Happily, my place was out of that cyclone's path. Now you boys come and stay with me. We'll commence all over again. Perhaps the crops are not so badly ruined after all. Maybe we can get a good deal from them yet. So don't get discouraged.. Let's find just how things stand. Remember, boys, you have your claims yet, and they'll be worth something some day."

"Yes," replied George, "the title is about the only thing the cyclone left, and I don't know as we can find the papers to that," he added, as he surveyed the mounds of dirt where the cabin had stood.

And the little trunk, with all his books and writings, would he find them again? he said.

Then, like a flash, there came to his mind the meeting that night between the Indian boy and himself. Nearly a month had elapsed since then. Why had he never opened the Indian boy's papers, and found out what it was he was so anxious for him to hear? His conscience seemed to reprove him for neglecting some duty that had come to him and he had failed to perform.

"Oh, well," he thought, "it was lucky I placed them where I did. My trunk has probably landed in some neighbor's cornfield, and we'll find it all right."

But cyclones have a way of blowing things into mysterious places, and days and weeks and months went by before any trace was found of the treasured books and papers.

.

.

CHAPTER VII.

NEW LIFE AND NEW HOPE.

THE boys went to work with a will, living with Maynard until they could get things in shape again, and by the time a month had passed their claims were restored to their former appearance. The crops had survived to some extent, and when the harvest came about one-third of what would have been secured was the fruit of their first summer's farming.

Autumn came at last. The rich, green tint of the prairie grass had a month before faded away, leaving a lonesome-looking landscape,—wide, vast, and desolate. Overhead great flocks of wild geese went coursing to the south, uttering their long, wild cry. Flocks of prairie chicken haunted the deserted cornfields, the boys setting traps in several places to which the wild fowl often fell victims.

November arrived, and with it the first blasts of approaching winter. A stiff "nor'-wester" set in one day, and the boys looked out with apprehension upon the snow coming down like a great white wall on the earth. They had made a trip to Prairieton and came home with provisions and clothing secured in exchange for some of the products of their claims, and were comfortably provided for; but they knew full well the perils of a winter on the frontier and looked forward to the coming months with anxiety.

The impulse to abandon their claims altogether, which came upon them at times, was never greater than just then, and a whole day was spent discussing some plan that would release them from their lonely surroundings.

"It's an easy matter to get into a trap," said Paul, "but another thing to get out. I don't know how we can get away from here now unless we walk."

"And it's three hundred miles to Omaha," observed George.

"And the walking isn't very good, either," added Paul. "Say!" he continued, casting his eyes over his patched and rough-looking clothes, "I wonder what people would think if we dropped into a place once more where civilization exists, looking as we do now?"

"Oh, they'd think the proverbial wild men of Borneo were loose again," replied George, "and probably run us out on general appearances."

"We might get an engagement with Buffalo Bill's Wild West Show as the long-haired boys from the far West," said Paul, laughing.

"That suggests something," said George. "Suppose we remove this thick and tangled brush from our heads for a change."

And so saying he hunted up an old pair of shears, once the property of Maynard, and began sharpening them on a whetstone. Paul was the first to submit to the shearing process, and seated himself on a stool with an old blanket around his neck.

"How do you want this job done,—by the acre?" asked George, as he ran his fingers through the heavy mass of hair on Paul's head.

"Oh, by the acre or by the week," replied Paul.

George had just begun his work, and the boys were in the midst of a lively conversation when they were startled by a rap on the door.

"Heaven!" exclaimed Paul, "this is a nice predicament to catch a fellow in," at the same moment throwing aside the blanket and hastily reaching for his hat, which he placed on his head so as to cover his partly-cut hair.

He was greatly relieved, though, when the door was opened and a lad belonging to a neighboring family entered.

"Father was over to Prairieton yesterday," he said, "and he brought this letter to you," handing a missive to George.

"A letter for me!" exclaimed George. "Now, I wonder who would write to me."

Hastily opening the envelope, he ran his eyes over the letter. As he did so a bright look spread over his face and in another instant he was all excitement.

"Hurrah!" he exclaimed, fairly dancing in the air, "the tide has turned at last. Good luck once more looks us in the face. No more——"

"What is it?" interrupted Paul, impatient to hear the good tidings.

"The best piece of news I've had for a long day. Read that," he said, handing Paul the letter, which the latter took and read aloud.

"Prairieton, Nebraska, November, 188—.
"Mr. George Eldredge:

"Dear Sir,—I have decided to return East and remain during the winter, and wish to secure a reliable person to take charge of my paper while I am away. I want to leave as soon as I can get matters settled, and would like to see you this week if you can arrange to come over. Come at once, if possible.

"Yours respectfully,

"J—— H——."

"Don't you remember," said George, "that is the old fellow we saw setting type in the 'Herald' office, on our first day in Prairieton?"

Paul gave the letter back to George, but was silent for a moment, and then said, rather sadly,—

"That's good news for you, George, but—but—what am I going to do?"

All George's merriment vanished.

"Oh, Paul," he said, "I had forgotten you. Forgive me for my selfishness——"

"Stop," Paul interposed, "I am the selfish one, not you. Here's a chance come for you to lift yourself a little out of adversity, and I must spoil it all because I am not as fortunate."

"Not a bit of it, old fellow," replied George; "but we'll not discuss that matter now. I'll go over to Prairieton to-morrow, and see what can be done, and then we will decide on what will be the best for us both."

The boys resumed their hair-cutting, Paul putting some finishing touches to George's head so that he would possess a presentable appearance, he said, when he stood in the presence of the august being who presided over the editorial columns of Prairieton's weekly newspaper.

Early the next morning, after a long restless night, that brought little sleep to his excited brain, George set out over the desolate prairie.

CHAPTER VIII.

BRIGHT DAYS AND DARK ONES.

GEORGE had expected to return to his claim within a day or two, but when he reached Prairieton he found the proprietor of the printing-office anxious for him to assume the duties at once, so that he would be fully posted on the affairs of the paper when left alone with its charge. And so a bargain was made by which George was to receive ten dollars a week, and entered upon his work the day after his arrival. Before the week was over he wrote to Paul, giving him a full account of his first experiences on a frontier newspaper, and telling him that he would come over to the claim the first day possible. Two weeks later the proprietor of the paper went East, and left George duly installed as manager, editor, and composing force of the same.

As delays are dangerous, and he wished to hold his claim, George had his pre-emption papers changed to a homestead filing, this arrangement giving him six months' time before again taking up his residence on it.

A spell of warm weather, remarkable for that time of the year, setting in, he drove over to the claim one day. Finding everything deserted, and rightly conjecturing that Paul was over to Maynard's, he kept on to the latter's cabin. What a royal welcome he received! To the two boys it seemed as though their separation had been for months instead of four short weeks.

"I've had a stroke of luck, too," said Paul, at the supper-table. "Yesterday Plimpton was over to see me about going to work on his ranch, and, although there will be some hard rustling, I jumped at the chance, and will start in to-morrow. It isn't very far from here, you know, and I can see to our claims right along, and keep things in order."

"I thought you boys had had enough of the claim business," chuckled Maynard.

"Well, it does get a little monotonous sometimes," said Paul. "Especially when a cyclone comes along and scoops everything off, and even takes part of the earth's surface. But, then," he added, "we will probably have better success next year. Another year is going to make a great change in this country."

In which prediction there was more than he imagined.

In the conducting of a little frontier paper our young editor found little out of the commonplace, but his vocation gave him an opportunity to cultivate what talent he possessed for writing. He was a close reader, too, and the evenings, dreary enough on the outside, were passed away in his humble office till a late hour over some book full of value to his mind. But when the strong, swift gusts of wind swept in from the prairies and rattled every building in the settlement, he often thought of Paul out on the ranch, and of the exposure he must at times be undergoing while guarding the cattle under his care. Then he would long for the time when spring would come, and when they could be together once more, and begin anew their work on the claims.

Spring came, and with it many of the settlers who had gone East the fall before, eager to once more take up their pioneer life. Among the first to appear was the proprietor of the paper, whose first move was to induce George to remain with him, as he found the latter's connection with the paper had brought it to a standing it never possessed before.

But George had made up his mind to return to his claim, as we know, and, settling up his affairs at the office, started at once for his former home.

He was joined a week later by Paul, and the spring work of the farmers' life commenced.

By the middle of May everything was in fine condition. The money earned during the winter had been invested in a team of Indian ponies, a plough, and some other farming implements. A few head of stock had been secured from Plimpton, a neat sod-barn erected a short distance from the cabin, and, though there was now but little money left, the boys considered themselves kings as compared with their condition the summer before.

But now an unforeseen event suddenly came into, and threw a cloud over, the lives of the young claim-holders.

Ever since his return from the ranch, Paul had not displayed the same robust constitution that had distinguished him the year before. Life in the saddle in the dead of winter, guarding a herd of cattle or in search of some heads that had strayed away before a "nor'wester," is enough to break down an iron constitution, and when the winter had worn away it was found that the strain had been too great for the young herdsman. Yet he bore up at first, hoping that the spring-time and warm weather would bring back his health and strength.

"Look here, old fellow," George would sometimes say, "I believe you are working too hard out here;" and then he would help Paul along with some task he had undertaken.

Paul would only laugh, and reply, "Oh, I'm all right; just a little indisposition that comes on occasionally."

The two boys were sitting by the cabin door, one evening, and George's thoughts had taken him back to the East.

Suddenly he roused from his reverie and, looking about him, said,—

"What a beautiful night it is, Paul!"

There was no answer.

"I say, Paul, what are you thinking about?"

Still no response.

Startled, he went over to where Paul was sitting, or had fallen rather in a half-reclining position against the wall. The moonlight poured full in his white, upturned face.

"Why, Paul, what's the matter?" cried George, taking the limp hands in his trembling grasp.

Another moment he was bathing the pallid face. Suddenly the eyes opened rather dazed-like, and then Paul rose to his feet.

"Why, George," he said, "what—what—has happened? Why, I—I—oh, I remember now. Oh! there is such a pain here," he continued, as he placed his hands to his head.

"There, dear old fellow," said George, tears filling his eyes; "you're all played out. That's what's the matter with you. I knew it all along. Come in and lie down. Perhaps you will feel better after a while."

Leaning upon George, Paul passed into the house, saying, as he did so, "I'll be all right in the morning."

CHAPTER IX.

LIGHT IN DARK PLACES.

THE morning came, but found the sick boy no better. Going over to Maynard's, George informed him of Paul's illness and of his intention of going to Prairieton for a doctor. He waited until the next day, hoping the case was not so serious and there would be an improvement; but as none came he started for the settlement, leaving Paul under Maynard's care.

The result was, Paul was pronounced to be suffering from a fever likely to become very serious, and the doctor expressed his regret at the great distance from the boys' claims to the town.

"He will need all the care that can be given him, and I shall come over again before the week is out," he said, when starting away.

In the course of a few days Paul's condition had become alarming. Failing to recognize either George or Maynard, he tossed about in delirium, calling some names now and then unknown to the two, of friends or relatives, perhaps, in his far Eastern home.

We will not linger over the sick-bed scenes that followed. For days the young sufferer's life hung very close to death. Painful days they were to George, but he kept up a brave heart, tenderly watching over the young life that he could not believe would be taken away.

As George sat by Paul's bedside, one day, trying to fight away the feeling of despair and of discouragement that at times now came upon him, suddenly it seemed as though he heard his own voice saying,—

> "Oh, tired friend, dear tired friend,
> Half-wishing all were at an end;
> Tired of the ceaseless, bitter strife;
> Of blighted hopes and a saddened life;

Do not despair, but toil along,
And lighten thy burden with a song;
For trial is often but the test
That wins for one the sweetest rest."

And then he thought he heard Paul saying again,—

"I think before we get through with our life out here we shall have full chance to live up to the spirit of your poem."

In another instant he had knelt down upon the earth floor of his little cabin.

"O God!" he said, "we leave this whole matter and this young life in Thy hands. Do as Thou seest best."

He arose, and went over to the table in one corner of the room. Some blank paper and a pencil were lying there. He sat down, wrote out the lines of the poem he had been repeating a few moments before, took another sheet and addressed it to a large publishing firm in a certain Eastern city. Folding the sheets carefully together, he said, "I wonder what they will think when they hear from me away out in this part of the world and under these circumstances."

Towards evening he went down on the flat lands bordering the creek to gather wood for a fire. As he searched along for this indispensable but rather scarce article in a country where trees do not grow except in little patches along the margin of some stream, he came upon a thick cluster of willow bushes growing so closely together that they almost defied invasion, but, making his way into the mass, he said,—

"I ought to find something in here. If there's nothing else, I'll cut down some of the largest willows and they'll burn for a while.

"Halloo! what's this?" he exclaimed in another moment, as he ran plump against a huge cottonwood log that stood in a half upright position, supported by the branches of its young neighbors all around it. "Here's a lucky find; but how in the world did it ever get in this spot? Looks as though the wind had crashed it down here some time or other, from the half-broken brush surrounding it."

He commenced hewing away, and for the time-being forgot the sick boy at home, forgot his own lonely surroundings, and as the strokes of his axe broke the stillness all around there also arose the notes of a whistler keeping time with the rhythmic sound. But suddenly the noise ceased, and if some one had happened along in that secluded spot just at that moment, the following words would have been heard, uttered in a high key,—

"Well—well—hip, hurrah! Here I've been slashing in this cottonwood and never noticed my little old trunk lying by the side of it, both blown over here, of course, on the day of that cyclone. It's lucky it was bound with iron clasps, or it never would have stood such a tumble as this. Here's my books, here's my writings,—yes, and, best of all, here's the roll of papers the Indian boy gave me."

CHAPTER X.

REAPING THE HARVEST.

PAUL was better. He had awakened to consciousness one day and recognized his two friends, George and Maynard, who were standing by the bed. From that day he continued to improve, and in a short time was able to sit up about the room. Then he ventured out one morning while George was away, and when the latter returned he asked, with a troubled look,—

"I say, George, what's become of the ponies? Must have loaned them to some of the neighbors."

"There, now," replied George, "you've been around investigating things early. Never mind about the ponies, Paul. We had to have a little money, and it was our only way to get it. It was a case of either losing you or the ponies, and so I chose the latter."

"Well," answered Paul, "we'll not mourn over the loss; but I don't know whether your choice was for the best or not."

"Paul," replied George, "we have just now been passing through a disheartening period, but let us hope there are better days in store for us. Life in this country has been too much for us. We ought to go now where there will be more rest and comfort than one can hope to find very soon in this land of hardship. Suppose we go to Prairieton, where I can probably secure my old position in the printing-office, and very likely you will find a clerkship in one of the stores. Then, after we have earned money enough, we might go out to some growing city in the northwest where there would be better opportunities. I know it seems hard to have to go from here after all that has been done. But look at the situation, besides, around us. Many of the settlers who came in here last summer had very little money, and were not as fortunate as ourselves in finding a way to tide over the winter. Spring found them almost destitute. How in the world they get along at all now is more than I can tell. Until they obtain relief, and the means are furnished them with which to improve their claims and carry on their work, and, above all, until a market exists for their products, there can be no advancement for the region. This can only be done through the help of capital. We want a railroad that will take our products to the markets in the State, and then we want men with money who will settle here, engage in business, build up the region, and thus create home markets, too. All this will occur as soon as the country attracts attention, and so, I say, it is hard to have to leave the place. But when will this be? And then there is another important matter that should keep us here."

Just then the door flew open with a bang, and Maynard, as the boys had never seen him before, hatless, his long white hair streaming in every direction, his clothing besmeared with clay and mud, dashed into the room, and, seizing first George and then Paul by the hands, he shouted,—

"Boys, there is gold in those hills across the river, and I've struck it at last. I've struck it rich; I've found enough to make us millionaires the rest of our days."

Yes, it was true. After days of patient searching, days of weary toil and striving that would have long before ended, had not the man been kept up by the one purpose,— that of helping the boys,—he had at last been rewarded, and now the help had come.

"This accounts for it all," said George, after the party had recovered from the flurry of excitement into which they had been thrown. "Many a time have I gone over to your claim, to find everything locked up and no signs of life. Why did you never tell us what you were doing,—what you were about?"

"Boys," replied Maynard, "I don't usually believe in secrets, but this I considered a justifiable one."

"But, say!" exclaimed Paul, suddenly, "what are we all thinking about, anyhow? Those hills across the river where this gold has been found is on the reservation and belongs to the. Indians. We have no right over there, and it would do us no good if the ground was strewn with diamonds."

"You're wrong there," answered Maynard, with a laugh; "you see, you fellows hav'n't kept posted on the news during Paul's sickness. Congress recently passed a bill purchasing the whole strip of land lying north of the river. The commission sent out to negotiate with the Indians have effected an agreement, and it now remains for the country to be thrown open to the white people. When this is done we can go over there and mine the region for all it's worth. But, George, what are you looking so glum about?"

While Maynard was speaking, George had gone to the window facing to the north, and stood looking earnestly at the long range of hills that now possessed such new and important interest to them.

Turning about, he said,—

"Over a year ago, when we stood upon that hill yonder for the first time, I spoke of the possibility of gold being there. I, as well as yourself, also alluded to the attitude we should bear, as Christian people, towards the Indians,—of the recognition we should show them when settling upon the land and developing its resources. The first has proven true. Shall not the second? You have not forgotten the band of Indians that strolled along here about a year ago. Among them was one—a young man—who had been taken to a training-school when a boy, educated and sent back to his people, but who had fallen back into their wild life and habits. The night before they went away from here he came to me and left a little roll of manuscripts. The papers became lost, and it was not until a few days ago that I found them. Now, suppose we read them."

CHAPTER XI.

THE INDIAN BOY'S MANUSCRIPTS.

HOW THE MESSIAH CAME TO THE INDIANS.

A STORY.

NIGHT had settled down upon an Indian village. Near the entrance to one of its smoke-stained lodges, two quaint-looking little children—an Indian boy and girl—sat upon the ground, looking with an expression of awe upon their dark faces at the moon, now big and full, so close to the earth, it seemed, one could almost touch it if standing upon the ridge that stretched along the eastern horizon.

"Where does the moon come from, anyhow?" asked the girl, suddenly.

"Why," replied the boy, "have you never heard? The Great Spirit made the moon to light the earth at night, and frighten away the evil spirits who go about doing bad when it is dark."

"But sometimes," said the little questioner, "it is only just so big" (indicating with her hands), "and is only a piece of a moon, every night getting larger until big and round like it is now, and then it begins to grow little again until it goes away altogether, and when it come back it is just like it was in the first place."

"Well, you see," the boy answered, "the Great Spirit works every night on the moon, adding a little until it is finished, and then goes to sleep. And while he is asleep the evil spirits come and eat a piece of it every night until it is all gone. And when the Great Spirit awakes and finds the moon gone, he has to begin over and make a new one again."

There was a moment or two of silence, and then the girl said, quite soberly,—

"Well, I should think the Great Spirit

would get tired of feeding the evil spirits on moons. Why don't he have a big brother or somebody to watch over the moon while he is asleep? It would be a great deal more sensible."

At this the boy became very angry, and, jumping up from the side of the girl, he stamped the ground and exclaimed,—

"Do you not know that it is wrong—wrong—to speak lightly of what the Great Spirit does? He will surely punish you for this."

He started away as if to leave her, but, looking back and seeing the girl had covered her face in dismay, as though something dreadful was about to happen, he paused, and as he did so the little one gazed up at him and said, with tears in her eyes,—

"Oh! oh! don't go away; I did not know I had said anything so terrible as that!"

The boy came back, sat down, and put his arms around the tiny form.

"Little sister," he said, "don't cry. No

one shall hurt you. The Great Spirit will not harm those who love and fear him. Only we must not speak lightly of what he does. It is enough for us to know that, whatever he does, he does for the best, and we must never question his works, however strange or mysterious they may appear sometimes to us."

In a little while her sobs had ceased, and, her composure again returning, the girl said,—

"Where did the first people come from?"

"The Great Spirit made them, of course," was the reply; "the Great Spirit made everything. He made the moon, and the sun, and the stars; and he made the earth and the people, and every living creature upon it,— the buffalo, and the deer, and the birds that fly in the air."

"But how——" How, where and when, and under what conditions was the world created, she was going to ask, but remembering what the boy had said the moment before, she covered her mouth with her hand, and said, presently, instead, "I mean where did the first people live?"

"Well," the boy answered, "the first people lived in the earth, but coming to a great opening one time that led outside, they came out and liked the new life with its light and sunshine much better than the old, and have ever since remained."

"Where do the people go to when they die?"

"To the happy hunting-grounds, where they live forever and ever, and where there is no pain or sorrow,—like it is in this life,—but where everybody is happy, and everybody loves each other all the time."

The girl was silent for some time. Then she said,—

"Well, I can't see why there should be any pain or sorrow in this life, if everybody would just be happy and love each other all the time, instead of waiting until we get into the next one. It would be much more sensible, and, besides, there wouldn't be anything embarrassing or unnatural after we got into the next life. I believe that's the way the Great Spirit wants us to do. *It is better to love than to kill.*"

For once the boy's gravity was disturbed and he burst into a laugh. Kissing the upturned face, he said,—

"Truly, a child's reasoning is, after all, the only real philosophy."

Which was a remarkable expression for a young man over whose head ten summers had hardly passed; but he spoiled it all by adding, "yet it is so impracticable among grown-up folks."

And it was so like the older world in which he lived.

So, a moment later, when the eyes—which had been so big and round from questioning, but now began to grow heavy—looked up at the boy again, and the little girl murmured, "Sing me something, brother," the boy took the child in his arms, and, as she nestled closely to him, there broke the stillness that brooded all around, the voice of one singing a warrior's song, the voice of one to whom there had just come from childish lips the gospel of love,—of peace, and not war. Over and over the voice sang these words:

> "We devote our bodies to the fight,
> And charge with the speed of eagles;
> We are willing to lie with the slain,
> *For then our name will be praised.*" *

Presently, seeing that the child had gone fast asleep, he entered the lodge, and laying the little form down on a blanket, covered it over snugly. Then he went outside and looked down the street of the village. A short distance from where he stood a group

---

* For the picture of wild Indian life here presented, the Indian's theory as to the origin of the moon, the belief that the people once inhabited the interior of the earth, and this song which the Indian boy sings, I am indebted to a volume published over twenty years ago by George P. Belden, who had spent twelve years among the Sioux, and General James S. Brisbin, of the United States Army.

of Indians were gathered about a camp-fire, listening to an aged warrior who stood in their midst and was telling them, as he had over and over before, of the glory of the once powerful Dakotas,—how, at one time, they composed a mighty nation, rich in their possessions of lands and ponies, but how they had become divided; how the tribes had wandered from each other; how the nation had fallen into decay, and how at last they were all fast disappearing before the approach of a wonderful race of white people from the East. "Once," he said, "we were free to do as we pleased. The Great Spirit gave us these lands to live upon and stocked it with games of all kind, with the buffalo, the antelope, and the deer. But the white man has taken our lands, the game is fast going away, and soon there will be nothing left but death for the Great Spirit's children. Has the Great Spirit forsaken his own? Is he less mighty than the white man, and can he not avenge the wrongs done his children? Listen, my warriors; the

Great Spirit has not forsaken us. He has turned from us but a little while, because we have warred against each other, because we have done wrong in his sight. Soon he will come back again. Soon there will rise up amongst us a mighty chief, who will be a Messiah to his people. He will be the Great Spirit himself in the form of man. And he will destroy the white people and give back to his children their lands, and then the buffalo and other game will come back in vast numbers, and, more wonderful still, all who have died will be restored to life, and the Dakotas will be no more weak and despised, but strong and mighty while they remain undivided and at peace with each other."

When the old man had ceased speaking, and when the members of the circle had gradually withdrawn and left the aged prophet huddled before the smoking embers of the dying camp-fire, the boy crept to his side and said,—

"Father, when will this Messiah come?

Why does he stay away from his children now, at all, when we need him so much?"

As he was speaking, a cold, hard glitter, that spoke of fanaticism, came into the old man's eyes.

"Listen, my child," he replied; "the Messiah has come. He is already here. But he is now only a boy. The prophets have foretold that in this day a child would be born among the Dakotas. And when he should hear of the coming of the Messiah he would at once go far to the West,—to a spot in the mountains where no man has yet been,—and there he should remain, and in due time the Great Spirit will reveal himself to the boy, and the boy will return to his people a full-grown man, with all the strength and power of the Great Spirit within him, and he will do all the things I have spoken of. Does the young brave understand? Do not ask me more, but go to your lodge and consider what I have said."

Slowly the boy walked away, overcome by

conflicting emotions. "The prophets have foretold that in this day a child would be born among the Dakotas," and this child was to be a saviour to his people. Who was that child? Why had the aged father said so meaningly, "Does the young brave understand? Do not ask me more, but go to your lodge and consider what I have said?" Was he that child? The very thought made him afraid at first. Then, he thought, how could he go away and leave his people,—his little sister, whom he loved so dearly? "But in due time the boy will return to his people a full-grown man, with all the strength and power of the Great Spirit within him." Somehow, although he had often wished that he were a man, the transition from boyhood into manhood in this case seemed altogether too sudden and under rather unnatural conditions, and the promise brought very little satisfaction to his mind. But if all that the father had said were true, and if, indeed, he were the child, how could he again look the old man in the face, who had so often patted him on the head and called him a mighty chief, destined to be some day a great man among his people? And, finally, when he thought of the condition into which his race had fallen,—fast drifting into utter helplessness and hopelessness, as it seemed to him,—he crushed down all his doubts and fears, and, looking up at the stars, exclaimed,—

"O Great Spirit, if I may serve Thee and my people, do with me as Thou will. I will do anything to help save them from the fate that Thou alone can avert."

An hour later, had the aged prophet of the tribe stepped out from his lodge, he might have seen a little figure mounted upon a pony fast flying across the prairie towards the West.

On the afternoon of a burning, stifling day, a wretched-looking white man came out on a high ridge stretching along the southern edge of a vast plain in the Sioux territory, and looked down upon a sparkling stream rippling musically along over its pebbly bottom. He had strayed away from a party of emigrants, and for days had wandered over great stretches of desert land, coming to long ranges of sand-hills, beyond which some cruel mockery would always say that help would be found, that life surely existed,—perhaps a pioneer's cabin or a stockman's ranch, or a settlement that pioneers had made,—only to reach the summit and look ahead, and see nothing but a great desolate expanse like that he had just left behind. He had thus wandered along until, starving and completely exhausted, he was ready to sink down for the last time. But the sight of water gave him new life, and, rushing down the steep declivity, he flung himself by the side of the current, burying his hot face in the stream and drinking great draughts of the sweet cool water, only to soon find that the relief was temporary, that a dying, burning thirst had come upon him which could not be quenched. Then he lay quietly on the bank a moment, and looked up at the blue sky overhead; but the sun burned his haggard face blacker, and, turning towards the stream, he lay for a while and listened to the water as it swished along beside him. Suddenly he started up with a wild cry as a strange feeling —he could not tell what it was, only that it seemed to speak of terror—came over him, and he dashed towards the top of the hill; then everything about him seemed whirling around and around, and then all became darkness.

When he looked up again the sun had gone down, and it was twilight.

"I have been asleep," murmured the man. "Such a bad dream I have had! Oh, no; it was not a dream. I remember now; I have been lost—so long—so long. How strange everything seems about me. I think—I think —I wonder if I am not going to die? O God, dear God,—do not let me die here alone, so far away from everybody, from everything."

He raised up a little and rested on his elbow.

As he did so, he uttered a faint cry, half of fear, half of thankfulness.

But a short distance away, looking straight down upon the helpless man, stood an Indian boy of ten or twelve years.

The man beheld an exultant expression upon the boy's face at first, but in another instant it had changed to one of pity. His wretched appearance, he thought, must have touched the boy's heart; but he did not know that just as the boy was about to slay the hated being of another race, the voice of a little sister came ringing in his ears,—"*It is better to love than to kill!*"

Coming forward and bending over the half prostrate man, the Indian boy said,—

"I speak English. The aged father, the prophet of our tribe, he speaks English. He teach me how. I will help you."

"God bless you, little man," replied the man, in a weak voice, "but I—I—do not want help now. It is too late."

"Ah, you are weak. You want food. I

will bring you some. Off there"—indicating with his hand—"are my people. If they find you, they kill—kill."

"My little friend," said the man, "it is of no use now,—I am going fast away. But—do not—do—not—leave me here to die alone. Stay but a little while; it will not be long."

The dying man stretched out a thin white hand in the darkness that had now settled down on the spot, and presently it rested on the little object crouching at his side.

"My little friend," he continued, "we are very foolish to fight and kill each other. Are we not brothers? Are we not alike? When all is sorrowful around the white man, does not his heart become heavy? When grief comes into the Indian's presence, does his soul not cry out in anguish? Are not our emotions, our feelings, then, alike? Yes; we are all as one. Long ago we wandered away from each other, from the one Great Father who placed us here. Now we have forgotten each other. We do not understand each other now. Hatred has come into our hearts, and we shed each other's blood. Listen, my little brother. The Great Father weeps at all this; his heart bleeds for his children who have gone so far away from each other and from him. Once he sent a Saviour into the world to bring them all back to him again. When this Saviour was born the angels came down from heaven and filled the sky with radiant light, and sang, 'Peace on earth, good-will to men.' This Saviour, my little brother, came into the world to take the hatred out of our hearts and replace it with love. While yet a boy, no older than yourself, he astonished everybody with his wisdom and sweet disposition. When he became a man he went about and made sad hearts happy, and men who had hated each other before began to love one another when he came among them. And though he went away, his Holy Spirit still remains, shedding abroad in men's hearts the love of the Heavenly Father. Some day white men will come to you and tell you of this Saviour, and if you are wise you will believe all they say to you. No, no, we must not kill each other. It is very wrong; it is very wicked. *It is better to love than to kill.* We must not hate each other. It should be love, and not hate. 'Love one another,' was what the Saviour said."

All became quiet. The Indian boy bent closer down by the speaker and waited eagerly for him to continue. But the man never spoke in this world again. The angel of death had come and taken his soul away.

For hours the Indian boy sat by the dead man's side. Into his heart there had crept a deep longing for the Saviour he had just heard about, and he wanted to learn more of him. Again and again he repeated the man's words, "While yet a boy, no older than yourself, he astonished every body with his wisdom and sweet disposition. When he became a man he went about and made sad hearts happy, and men who had hated each other before began to love one another when he came among them."

Then, of a sudden, he jumped up and clapped his hands, and exclaimed,—

"Why, the aged father—the prophet of our tribe—has made a mistake. I must hasten back to him and to my people, and tell them of this, the real Messiah, who has already come."

So this was how the Messiah came to the Indians.

———

Among the people whose lodges are thrown up around you, to-night, an Indian boy was born. Among them his young life was spent. In his childhood he was as other Indian boys. He knew of no world other than his own, save a mysterious land peopled with gods and the spirits of those who had lived and died on earth, an unknown region the story-tellers were wont to speak to him about. He was told of other races, strong and mighty, before whose approach his people were disappearing like darkness before the light of day. A chivalrous death, deeds of valor and of vengeance,—these were held up to him to be emulated,—the things that made true greatness, and upon all races which did not so believe he was taught to look with contempt.

That boy was myself.

One day some white men, who were not like any we had ever seen before, came and dwelt among us for a while, and when they went away they took many of the boys and myself with them. We were taken far to the east to a great city, and there we were placed in a large building, where we were told that a new life was to be shown us, where we were to be taught to become like the white people.

No sooner had I been so lifted up and the training-school had wrought a complete change in my being, than I became filled with ambition for noble attainment and to plan and dream over what my life would be. I said at first I would be a great man and win a name for myself, as had many I constantly read of in the white men's books. Then I said I would be a poet (for it seemed as though the power of a poet burned within me when I remembered my race), one who would cheer the hearts of his weary people with song. When the school-course had been completed, and my mind had been strengthened by the touch of Christian influence as well, I realized the responsibility attached to me,— plainly I saw what my duty was. I returned to my people. For a long time I tried to tell them what I had learned in the schools, tried to teach them to become like myself. Some listened and respected me. A few followed my example, but the majority laughed and taunted. Were they to be blamed so much, after all, when we remember that so many had been injured and degraded by the baser elements of civilization, and therefore unable, or, it may be, unwilling, to discriminate between the false and the true, they spurned the religion and the help of those who would be their true friends? I do not care to blame any one for what next followed; but, thrown among my old associates, trying to do a fruitless work, I grew doubtful and discouraged, and gradually the old spirit came upon me. Slowly I slipped back into the former life, until at last I forgot God, lost hope, ambition, plans and all, and have become as you see me now. To-night there has come back to me all the old longings,—the strength, the purpose that once was mine,—and there also comes this thought: already your race has found its way to the border of our lands, and how soon it will be when it shall have swept over and around our very homes! Now, the Indian has a human heart. He loves his people, his brothers, his little sisters. Home-life is sweet and dear to him, peculiar and imperfect though it may now be. As your race comes to us, then, why may it not yet bring to him its civilization and life? Why may not his home be made sweeter still,—purified and more perfect? There is a simple way by which this can be done,—through the power of love,—that kind of love the Saviour brought into the world,—Divine love, which is not checked by race or color, but draws all men into one common fellowship, and where men minister to each other's wants. My purpose is to do what I can among my people to make this possible, and why, in turn, may you not do the same with yours? This is my thought, and this is my reason for coming to you to-night. Shall we not meet as brothers,—no longer as foes?

CHAPTER XII.

AN OLD QUESTION AGAIN CONSIDERED.

THE act of Congress under which that part of the Sioux reservation lying north of the young claim-holders was opened to settlement, and which allotted to the Indians the remaining land in severalty, also giving them the rights of citizenship, made the carrying out of a splendid project possible.

The first step to be taken was a trip to the Indian agency, and all arrangements were being made for a departure for that place in the morning. Paul had gone over to the frontier post-office for any mail that might have come during the week, and Maynard and George were out in the barn brushing down one of the horses they had secured from a neighbor that forenoon.

"After all," said George, as he paused in the work, "perhaps we are a little too enthusiastic over this matter, forgetting that many have devoted long years towards solving the Indian question, as it is called, and have accomplished very little real apparent good. So many obstacles are encountered when one starts out to make true men out of any race of uncivilized people."

"Lord Macaulay once wrote," replied Maynard, "'it is the nature of man to overrate present evil and to underrate present good, to long for what he has not, and to be dissatisfied with what he has. This propensity, as it appears in individuals, has often been noticed both by laughing and by weeping philosophers. It was a favorite theme of Horace and of Pascal, of Voltaire and of Johnson. We read in the most ancient of books that a people bowed to the dust under a cruel yoke, scourged to toil by hard taskmasters, not supplied with straw, yet compelled to furnish the daily tale of bricks, became sick of life, and raised such a cry of misery as pierced the heavens. The slaves were wonderfully set free. At the moment of their liberation they raised a song of gratitude and triumph; but in a few hours they began to regret their slavery, and to reproach the leader who had decoyed them away from the savory fare of the house of bondage to the dreary waste which still separated them from the land flowing with milk and honey.' It is also the nature of man to look on the bright side of things, instead of the dark; to learn to be satisfied and patient, whatever his condition, which the 'most ancient of books' teaches, if it teaches anything. But let us not forget to make allowance for this element of discontent in human nature Macaulay has so happily touched upon, that will surely exist, no matter what remedies we may apply for the solution of the Indian question. Now, let us consider the case of the Indians, beginning first with a simple little illustration. You remember that last spring we set out two hundred young trees on Paul's tree claim, and we expect to have quite a piece of timbered land there some day. But we did not make one of the trees, did we? We could only make the conditions favorable for the tree's existence, setting it out properly and giving it all the care needed until its roots should take firm hold into the soil. Now the rain feeds it, the sun warms it, and, nurtured by all the forces of nature around it, it is growing into a thing of natural life itself. Transplanting men from barbarism to civilization is a great deal like transplanting trees from one soil to another. The best results, of course, are to be with the child, the young sprout, rather than the man, the full-grown tree; but in either case we cannot make the man himself any more than we can make a tree. We can only make the conditions favorable for the man's existence. So in the doing of this—in the solving of the Indian question—there are two fundamental rules to be observed: 1. We must aid him to become prepared to enter civilized life, by the establishing of training-schools and proper systems of government. 2. We must give him the rights of citizenship, and admit him to our society after such preparation has been completed. We have recognized the first rule in many instances, but, alas, for the second! Assuming just now, however, that we have done our part, the Indian must now do his. God has placed within every human being the power to become a man; he has put upon him certain obligations and responsibilities which must be recognized if he would become a man. He has endowed different men with different elements of genius, the development of which lies only with the possessor, and those things which make the real man,—whatever his capabilities may be,—such as character and manhood, why these can only be fashioned by the individual himself. So, then, there must be first a desire on the part of the Indian for civilization, a willingness to adapt himself to the new conditions that become thrown around him, and then a realization of the principles we have just stated, and last, but best of all, a determination to rely upon his own strength and not too much upon the strength of others.* But while man pos-

---

* I was talking with Rev. John P. Williamson, a Presbyterian missionary among the Sioux, in regard to a well-known young man of the Indian race, who was at the time of our conversation employed as a government physician among the Indians. "He is of the Santee tribe," said Mr. Williamson, in substance, "who formerly lived in Minnesota, where Redwood now is. When the Minnesota massacre occurred, the Indians became scattered, and he was taken up to Manitoba, being then about six years old. When about twelve or thirteen, his father brought him back to the Yankton Agency, where the Santees are now living. Here he was placed in the Presbyterian boarding-school, which was in my charge, and it was then that he first came under my observation. A marked difference was at once to be seen between him and the other boys in the school. Life up in Manitoba, where the Indians are thrown on their own resources, had developed within him a more independent, self-reliant spirit, which, together with other natural

sesses these elements of independence, and is an individual by himself, just as the tree is a separate, distinct thing in the physical world, he needs the lives of other men, he must come in contact with other men and possess their society and fellowship, just as the life and growth of the tree is dependent upon the other forces of nature,—air, rain, and sunshine. On this principle of association the weak become strong in the presence of the strong, and the human mind becomes developed and more comprehensive. This brings us, then, again to the second rule I have spoken of; and so let me ask how can we ever expect the Indians, whom we look upon as an inferior race of people, to make much progress, if we do not observe it and admit them to our society and companionship. And so, too, by the way, we ought to

---

ability, made him superior to the other boys, and without which—no matter what other good qualities one may possess—one cannot overcome and attain to what he has."

see the folly of placing the Indians upon reservations, where—whatever the other evils may be as a result, and about which we hear so much*—contact with the civilized races becomes impossible, and personal responsibility and independent manhood must perforce become eliminated from their nature. The reservation system of government may have its place when it seeks to carry out the first rule stated.; when it makes employment in the service possible for the Indians,† and

---

* While on a visit to the Pine Ridge Agency, last fall, I was informed that Captain Brown, acting Indian agent, had completely revolutionized the condition of things existing previous to the late troubles at that point, and was carrying out a policy of management that was meeting the approval of both the Indians and the white people. So the thought occurred to me that, after all, a great step towards solving the Indian question lay in the simple, old-fashioned remedy of having the "right man in the right place," and if civil service could be made of any avail, of keeping him there, after he had been secured.

† Much of the work about the agencies and on the reservation could be done by the Indians, instead of white

leaves opportunity for a proper degree of self-government;* and when it endeavors to instil into every mind the true spirit of civilization; but after the work has been accomplished the first rule must give way to the second, which offers them the civilization for which they have been prepared. If not, it would be just as reasonable to keep a lot of pupils in a school after their courses had been completed, keeping them prisoners for life, and never allowing them to crawl over the school-yard walls into the busy world outside. But we frequently hear the argument that the Indians can never be fully civilized, that they are incapable of imbibing the inspiration that characterizes other races, and we are pointed to various tribes in the East, such as the Seneca nation, whose reservation

---

persons; and especially could the educated Indians be employed as teachers and helpers in the boarding- and day-schools. Indeed, while at Pine Ridge I was told that the government was beginning to adopt this policy.

* See " Indians as Citizens," Appendix.

lies in western New York, and on whose lands the city of Salamanca, a community of white people, exists, and yet the Indians themselves, who have apparently had the benefit of civilization for years, have never, with the exception of a few individuals, made much comparative progress. If we look very closely into this particular case, however, we shall find that the Indians and the white people do not enter into each other's society. The Indians dwell in little huts along the banks of the Alleghany River, coming into town occasionally to sell their farm products and bead-work, being looked upon with curiosity while there; and whenever an Indian and a white person pass each other on the highway, the first invariably casts his eyes to the ground, or turns his face away and marches stoically by. How different the condition of these people might be, had there been a warm friendship and more affiliation between the two races in the past! Nay, let us not think that the Indians are an incapable, inferior people. Within many a rough shell a beautiful and priceless pearl is often found. Among these children of the prairie who can tell what pure and lofty sentiment exists, what mind may dwell that only needs to feel the touch of human sympathy and love to shine forth in all its power and become a blessing to mankind? Now, the greatest trouble has always been, as we find evidenced here on the frontier, that when we first come in contact with the Indians, forgetting that centuries of animal life have made him what he is, his whole appearance causes us to turn from him in disgust. The settlers, with but few exceptions, look upon him with suspicion and contempt, and hatred that becomes all the more intensified when fired by the feeling that he is being wronged, his spirit becomes aroused, and he takes up his work of inhuman atrocity. Again, we always judge the Indian race by its worst element, forgetting that upon the same principle we should have to call ourselves outlaws because of the horse-thieves and border ruffians that dwell among us, or that back East the people must all be irreclaimable because of the hardened criminals that fill our prison-houses. Somehow or other the 'advance guards of civilization' are its worst elements,—as a certain writer has observed, the outlaw and the whiskey-bottle, —and by the time the missionary gets along with his Bible the work has been done, the seeds of bitter prejudice have been sown, and reformation becomes almost impossible. Hence it is, as the Indian boy has implied, that, lied to, mistreated, and corrupted by unscrupulous white men, the Indians have often spurned the white man's religion and civilization. Having never as a race fully embraced the Christian faith and enjoyed the happiness that lies in a pure and perfect civilized life, they prefer the wild, free condition that has been theirs, where the Great Spirit is the ruler over all, and where a deep and intense love for the superstitious forms the faith and poetry of their lives. But, back of all these prejudices, back of all these questions of systems of government, of manhood, personal responsibility and independence, back of all I have mentioned, there lies another force upon which all these principles rest,—that of Divine love in human hearts. What is Divine love? Divine love is man's love for God. He who loves God loves all that he has created. The most insignificant, degraded being, still retaining the breath of God within it, appeals to his sympathy and love. So when this Divine love comes into our hearts, we, who had despised the Indian because of the uncivilized life that had made him repulsive to us, now come to love him, and we become filled with a desire to lift him up and place him upon an equal standing with ourselves. And so, too, when there comes into the Indian's soul the knowledge and love of the only one true God, his heart becomes transformed, and he no longer sees in the white people deadly foes, but friends and brothers.

And thus, you see, Divine love must come into our hearts first, and sweep away all these race prejudices and all the barriers that stand in the way, and the matter of solving the Indian question by the observing of the two rules I have mentioned will then become simple and easy enough."

"But the trouble is," said George, somewhat dryly, "Divine love is not common enough in the hearts of men, especially out here on the frontier; and now, too, that this wealth has come, will not its possession, as it usually does, make many cold and selfish, and make impossible the coming together of the races in the manner we have been talking about?"

"'The love of money is the root of all evil,'" replied Maynard; "but the possession of money is not of itself an evil. The evil depends upon the manner in which we obtain it, our *love* for it, and the uses to which we put it. Now, wealth has its legitimate place in the world. It is the fruit of industry, and its purpose should be to, in turn, give life to industry,—just as life creates life. You have probably seen by this time how necessary it is that we should have capital to help us in the advancement of this region. The gold that is stored away in those hills across the river may represent this capital,—the wealth in the East,—that is the product of our country's industry; and if a portion of it were out on its proper mission, that of creating enterprise and business in the West by natural and legitimate investment, instead of being used for selfish purposes at home, what a hum of industry and a time of prosperity would begin all over these out-of-the-way regions. I suppose that some of the settlers, having had a rough time of it, will now consider themselves privileged to get all the personal enjoyment they can, regardless of other people's condition; but if we do our part in this matter, I think you will see many others following our example."

"Let us look directly at the young Indians,

—the sprouts, as you call them," said George. " It has always seemed too bad to me, that in almost every instance where they go back to the agencies (and they never go anywhere else) from the schools, in a very short time they have fallen back into their old life and customs. For a long time I have been perplexed at this, and sometimes have been ready to believe, with many others, that such a thing as the elevation of the race is impossible. But I think I can see into it a little better now. The young Indian, after leaving school, finds himself in a trying position, and feels that he is looked upon as a peculiar personage, and out of place among the white people. In a world where there seems to be so much competition, and where so many seem unable to obtain a foothold, he sees then but little hope of his ever getting a start of any kind. So he returns to the reservation, sometimes for the purpose of helping his people in some way, but more often because of love for his own kind and a longing for the companionship which there awaits him, and which he cannot find anywhere else. Back again at the agency he finds but little to do,—no employment or opportunity for being industrious. In his Christian life he receives but little encouragement from his own people. It is seldom that he comes in contact with any Christian white person, aside from the missionary who may be stationed among the Indians. The white people who visit the agencies usually come out of curiosity, to hunt out some of the noted Indian characters they have heard and read about; to behold the Indian in his native state; to load themselves down with his handiwork, and then to go away—to write a book, perhaps, or a long article for their home newspaper about 'Lo! the poor Indian; how he lives,' but more often on how he don't live. No thought is given to the Christian young Indian, who might have been helped so much by a word of encouragement, or a little friendly recognition from these same people, as well as the settlers who live nearer to him. A man is largely what his environment is. With but little to elevate him, and everything tending to drag him down, what wonder is it that he so often falls back into the old condition?"

"As a man needs the companionship of others," answered Maynard, "so, too, is he very apt to be what his society is; yet, wherever that society is at fault, the individual, strengthened and quickened by God's Holy Spirit, may be the very opposite to those around him, and, instead of being influenced by his surroundings, may often draw others unto himself, and bring his surroundings up to his own standard. Whatever may be the condition of things in civilized communities, it need have no bearing upon the educated Indian's case. His province lies at home, where, in the advancement of his race, his services will be of incalculable value,—in fact, indispensable.* We have been observing the

---

* Under the instruction of one of his own race, it would seem that an Indian would make better progress than

first rule that I mentioned by the establishing of training-schools for a good many years, until now there is no telling how many of these educated Indians there are upon the different reservations. It seems as though the time had come, at least where in close neighborhood to the white communities, that the second rule should now be carried out, and that the Indian should enter citizenship and become a part of our society. The law that Congress has just passed makes this possible——"

"Pardon me for interrupting," said George, "but I understand that this law does not give the Indian a clear title to his land until twenty-five years have elapsed,—the best part

---

beneath a white person. The first would certainly better understand the nature, and know just the needs of, and take a deeper interest in lifting up one of his own people, and inspire in them a greater disposition to advance; while both would be more apt to possess each other's confidence and friendship,—a very necessary relationship that should exist between two parties trying to accomplish anything, and which is too often lacking under any other condition.

of a life,—and even then the President has the power to further extend the time, and that all the moneys derived from sales of his surplus property are deposited in the United States Treasury for the same period, the principal and interest being appropriated from time to time by Congress for his benefit. It seems to me that this is not so much of an improvement upon the old system, after all. He simply continues on a ward of the government, under different conditions, only with the prospect of breaking the final chain of bondage, if he can hold out another quarter of a century. We are told that this arrangement will throw a wall of safeguard around him against unscrupulous white men, and that by the time he comes into the full ownership of his property, the conditions shall have become changed, and he will be more able to assume the responsibility of owning a thing himself. There may be something in this argument where it applies to many of the Indians, but here is where we again fall into the common error of treating them all alike. When this measure was being debated in Congress, the question arose as to whether or not it should apply to the five tribes more civilized than the others, and it was the sense of nearly all the members of that body that it would be an outrage to include them within its provisions. Now, the same might be said as to many individuals in all the other tribes,— these educated ones whom we have been talking about,—from whom it would be quite as unjust to deprive the highest privilege of citizenship,—that of the right of ownership in land and its value."

"Rome was not built in a day," replied Maynard. "Neither do complete reforms come at a single bound, however much we would like to have them. Whatever there may be defective in this measure, it can only be best learned by putting the law into operation, and then remedied by further acts of legislation. As the law now stands, any individual Indian can take a fee-simple to a certain quantity of land, sufficient for him to make a living upon, and become a citizen of the United States. Whenever a majority of all the male Indians on any reservation desire it, the reservation can be abolished, and the lands allotted in severalty to them; and as soon as the allotment is made the allottee becomes a citizen of the United States, and the law protects him as it does any other citizen. 'While he does not receive a full patent to his land at first, the same is made inalienable and non-taxable,' as a member of Congress has expressed it, 'for a sufficient length of time for the new citizen to become accustomed to his new life; to learn his rights as a citizen, and prepare himself to cope on an equal footing with any white man who might attempt to cheat him out of his newly-acquired property.' This law, however, brings about a new system that is a vast improvement on the old one, as it abolishes the reservation, and establishes a condition where personal responsibility and citizenship becomes possible, and where, best of all, the two races may be brought more in contact with each other. Now, in this present case, as the Indians whom we are directly interested in take the first step necessary, we should stand ready to do our part and welcome them to our society. The purpose of wealth, besides, I have said, is to create industry. Upon industry depends the existence of mankind, and the Indian, like the rest of humanity, must have something to do. With the wealth that has come into our possession, we, too, can help to make this possible, aiding him in more ways than one, and not simply look upon this as a matter to be settled by the Indian and the government alone." *

"But gold-mines are not to be found at every turn," said George, smiling, "and I

---

* See " Indians as Citizens," Appendix.

should not be surprised, after all, if many of the Indians at this point should hesitate about entering citizenship. And more so, because much of the land in the reservation is not one flowing with milk and honey; on the contrary, it runs more to sand than anything else, and it is not the best in the world for farming. There is but little market for anything that might be raised, anyhow, and as the new step would mean the severing of all tribal relationship, the doing away of long-established forms and customs, and the giving up of many claims upon the government, it is very likely that few would care to exchange their present condition for the one proposed."

"I have already spoken of the general good that would come to all by our maintaining the proper relationship that should exist between man and man," replied Maynard, "and if this is observed to the letter the severing of tribal relationship and the doing away of old forms and customs would only

mean the bringing in of a new condition,—
the one which the Indian boy is so anxious his
people should possess,—where the Indian's
home-life would still be retained, purified,
and made more perfect. There was once a
time, and not very long ago, either, when
the greater part of this State where we now
are was included in the great American
Desert, and regarded as worthless, arid
wastes of land; but when immigration entered
upon it, although there were many sandy
regions, plenty of available territory was
found that is now covered with thrifty farms
and towns. So it will be with the land on
the reservation. But as it required long
days, and years, too, of hard toil and privation to make our best regions what they
are, so will there have to be, in many cases,
first, the same expenditure of energy, and
the undergoing of trial and sacrifice, in the
building up of all this new country. The
better things in this world are only obtained
at a cost, and the things most appreciated

are those for which there has to be a struggle. And the best manhood is that which is moulded by such experience, and has within it the elements of independence, of ruggedness, and of will. I think," concluded Maynard, with a smile, "that two young men, not a thousand miles from here, have learned this lesson well during the last year, and it would be a good thing if every young Indian, as well as every other young man, could go through the same experience."

The clatter of horses' hoofs was heard coming along the bottom-lands from the direction of the post-office, growing louder and nearer until a horse dashed around the corner of the barn and came to a halt, and Paul, once more the picture of health, and his face flushed for the moment from the ride, dismounted.

"Here's some important mail for you, George," he said, coming forward and handing him a long envelope that bore the name of Barton Brothers, publishers, in the upper left-hand corner.

Tremulously George tore away one end, and drew out a letter, the reading of which sent his blood to fever-heat:

"OFFICE OF BARTON BROS., PUBLISHERS.
BOSTON, August —, 18—.

"MR. GEORGE ELDREDGE:

"DEAR SIR,—We are well pleased with your work. Enclosed find check for seventy-five dollars for same. Surprised to hear from you in that part of the world. Have talked the matter over with Henry Barton, and we have decided to offer you the associate editorship of our monthly magazine, *The Literary Review*. Let us hear from you as soon as possible.

"Yours very truly,
"ROBERT BARTON."

The poem he had sent away while Paul was sick had been accepted, and that Robert Barton, junior member of the firm of Barton Brothers, publishers, should make him such an offer as this,—he could hardly believe it.

A light burned late in the young claim-holders' cabin. Paul and Maynard had long since gone to bed, hoping to get a good night's rest before the start for the agency in the morning; but why does George still sit by the side of the rough table, looking pale, and with an unnatural, burning brightness in his eyes, and why every few moments does he start up and pace the floor in a troubled manner?

"After all," he is saying, "this may be a delusion. This gold find may prove, as often is the case, of no account. And then what? Just where we were before,—without much money, without help, almost without hope. The check I have just received will take Paul and me both East. Once there, once deep in the work that has been so long dear to my heart, who can tell what a bright record I may make for myself? Yes, I'll——"

He stopped suddenly, as though something sharp had stung his conscience, just as he had done several times before.

"But how can I leave him?" he said; "his thoughts and motives were so like my own."

He went over to his little trunk, and opening it, took out the Indian boy's manuscripts.

"Yes, here are the lines," he said, presently. "'I would be a great man, I said at first, and win a name for myself, as had many I constantly read of in the white men's books. Then I said I would be a poet (for it seemed as though the power of a poet burned within me when I remembered my race), one who would cheer the hearts of his weary people with song.' The poet and the writer have their place in the world," he said, as he rolled the papers up and put them back in the trunk; "and their greatest mission is to cheer the hearts of their weary people with song."

He went to the door and stepped out. The sky was one mass of stars. As he looked up a tiny orb swept through the heavens and left a long trail of fire for a moment in its wake.

"But so much for selfish fame," he added, "seeking only that its name shall be praised.

Like the shooting-star, it may trail its brightness before the minds of men for a little while, and then it dies out and is heard of no more. I shall wait awhile. There is other work for me to do here. The boy waits for me among his people. I will go to him."

For a long time he stood, his arms folded, immovable. Then suddenly he breathed out these words:

> " Why, who would strive for fame or gain,
> When so much darkness, tears, and pain
> Weigh down on human souls?
> 'Twere better far to live unknown,
> Aye, share awhile the humblest home,
> Where dwelleth struggling human souls,—
> If such are pointed to the light
> That leadeth out of darkest night,
> And guideth every human soul,—
> Who, looking into brighter skies,
> Shall find no longer death, pain or sighs,
> But life and hope for every soul."

CHAPTER XIII.

CONCLUSION.

THE day for the distribution of cattle to the Indians had come again. Over at the corral, a mile from the agency, where the government herd was quartered, everything was being made ready for the issue. Government officials superior gave orders here and there, and government officials subordinate hastened to obey them. Indians of all sizes, ages, and description—from the little "pappoose," who looked over his mother's shoulder, and blinked curiously out of his little eyes, to the scarred old veteran of the plains, the noblest Roman of them all, who, wrapped in his government toga, deigned to take but a passive interest in what was going on about him—were gathered around the entrance to the enclosure in groups, chatting, and waiting patiently for the issue to commence. The ones who had been selected to receive the cattle were mounted on horseback and equipped with Winchester rifles, wearing belts around their waists well supplied with cartridges. Brightly attired, besides, in many instances, they rode to and fro, winning glances of admiration from the assemblage, and exciting the envy of the small-boy Indian, who for some reason or other seemed not to be included among those signalled out as objects for reformation in the boarding-school at the agency.

While the spirit of sociability and great expectancy thus brooded over the spot, a grave-looking old man mounted a wagon and commenced to pour out a harangue in a dry, monotonous tone of voice. It was the same old story he had to offer, the same old expression of discontent, the same old charges of mismanagement and unfairness on the part of the government in its dealings with the Indians. In a few moments he was surrounded by a group of auditors who listened eagerly to all that he had to say. No sooner had he ceased speaking than another took his place. The second person, unlike the first, was of the nervous, emotional character, and commenced to talk rapidly and ramblingly, emphasizing his words with many wild gestures. It was observable, too, that he made no impression upon the listeners, who only shook their heads at each other with a smile and gradually withdrew, until very soon the poor fellow was addressing nothing but space.

"That man is a little crazy," said a bystander. "He isn't just right. He's full of schemes that's going to solve the Indian question and take the Indians all out of their troubles. But he's one of these fellows that catches on to the tail end of a movement or agitation of any kind after it is all over, and clings to it with the ardor and enthusiasm of the most earnest advocate of anything. It appears now that all the rations for the

Indians upon this reservation used to be distributed entirely at this agency, on which occasion the Indians would be gathered in large numbers. This coming together always meant the holding of councils, the making of speeches, and the occurrence of incidents that only tended to create a dissatisfied spirit among the Indians. The government, in its effort to get the Indians more scattered and settled upon the reservation, and to discourage this spirit as much as possible, has separated the reservation into districts, with a sub-agency in each, and where the Indians of which now receive their rations. There was considerable opposition from the Indians, of course, at the time of the change, but it has all died out now, and everybody appears to be satisfied, excepting the old fellow we just heard. It seems," concluded the speaker with a laugh, "that he wants somebody to write a letter to the President at Washington, and see if something can't be done and the old system again established."

"Perhaps," remarked another by-stander, "he may not be such a fool as one might imagine. Many a fool turns out to be a genius in this world. Many a leader of a forlorn hope has proven a great benefactor to humanity by still clinging to that hope, after every one else had deserted it. However short-sighted or mistaken this individual may appear, he may be filling a place in the world by keeping alive a sentiment that will some day touch the hearts of those more able to see and understand and carry out just what should be to the best interests of his people."

The first speaker was a settler who lived in close neighborhood to the agency, and the second none other than George Eldredge, who, together with Paul and Maynard, had driven up to the corral that morning after a three days' journey from home and were now on their way to the agency.

Just as he spoke there was a commotion, indicating that the issue was to commence.

At the entrance to the corral, the mounted Indians had formed in two rows facing each other, making a gauntlet through which the cattle were to pass when coming out. The gate was thrown open. Inside the enclosure mounted horsemen commenced to halloo and beat the backs of the cattle. There was a sound of bellowing and the scraping of horns against the sides of the corral. Then a scared-looking animal appeared in the gateway, looked confused for a moment, and seemed disposed to retire from whence he came, but the herd was pushing behind, and retreat impossible. So he plucked up courage and dashed down between the two rows of horsemen, and started for the open prairie. As he did so a clerk, stationed in a little booth at the entrance, called out the name of an Indian. A figure darted away from one of the lines, and sped after the luckless animal. As he brought up by the side of his victim, he levelled his gun at him; there was a sharp report, then another, and then the animal stumbled and fell.* This was repeated, until in a few moments the prairie was swarming with cattle running in every direction, hotly pursued by the Indians.

In the course of an hour the issue was completed. Some of the Indians, instead of killing their cattle on the spot, urged them over the hills and drove them away, but the majority shot their game down and butchered it where it fell. Cutting the meat into long strips and piling it on the back of a pony, an Indian would start for home, pulling the animal along by a long rope tied to the halter.

Over at the agency, an hour after the issue, everything was animation in and around the trading-stores, where the Indians were arrayed in bright — and some not so bright — costumes, smoking cigarettes, and ranged along the counters, inspecting everything upon the

---

* At the Pine Ridge Agency this method of issuing cattle was discontinued several months ago.

shelves which the clerks would show them, and sitting around, shrouded in blankets, on the sidewalks outside. I suppose there was much going on to interest the average stranger, but Maynard and the young settlers took no note of it. They were too eager to find the object of their search, and when they reached the agency they drove at once to the Indian agent's head-quarters, in a long red wooden building, a few rods from the trading-stores. To their dismay, however, they learned that the agent had gone away to one of the sub-agencies, and would not be back until the next day. "There are so many cases of this kind," said the clerk, with whom they talked, "and as the boy did not give you his name, it would be better for us not to attempt to find him until the agent returns, who will help us and authorize us to make the search."

All that day George hung about the trading-stores, looking into the face of every young Indian he encountered, only to meet with disappointment each time. "People say," he once said to Paul, "that all Indians look alike; but that face, those bright eyes, why I will never forget how he looked that night. I could pick him out from among a thousand others."

Late in the afternoon he went down to the little hotel, where the party had concluded to stop while awaiting the agent's return.

His two friends had gone over to the boarding-school, the hotel-keeper told him, and left word for him to come over there and join them.

"I'm feeling a little tired out," said George, as he threw himself into a chair. "I guess I'll stay here until they get back."

He picked up a paper lying upon the table, but threw it down again a little later as an Indian entered at the office door and came rapidly towards him. George saw at once that it was the erratic one of the two speakers who that morning had been haranguing the Indians at the government corral. Coming forward until he stood directly before George, the Indian placed his hands upon his own lips, shook his head in a negative manner, then he made a circle around his heart, then raising his hand, he pointed directly upward. "Now, what in the world does he want?" thought George. "If the hotel-keeper had not stepped out he could tell all right. Oh, I have it. Touching his lips and shaking his head means that he cannot speak my language. Making a circle round his heart, pointing up to the heavens to the Great Spirit, probably means friendship, and very likely he wants me to write that letter to the great father at Washington." He took out his pencil and pointed to some paper on the table; but the Indian shook his head as if to say no. A pause followed. Then the Indian again went through the curious motions, and finally beckoned, as if to come. "He wants me to go somewhere," said George. "Well, I'll go and see what he wants." Passing out from the hotel, the two walked down the street of the agency until they came to a cluster of log-houses George had noticed as the party entered the agency that morning. Going up to the door of one of these the Indian entered, and, as George followed, a long object, lying upon a bunk in one end of the room and covered with a blanket, was the first thing that met his eyes. The Indian made long strides to the head of the bunk, and then turning around and facing George, but first again placing his fingers upon his lips, making a circle around his heart and pointing towards heaven, he drew aside the blanket, and there, with a stony cast upon his face and the brightness gone out of his eyes, lay the boy for whom the young settler had looked that day,—dead!—gone out of this world and into another, where it is good to believe that man is no longer arrayed against and misunderstands his fellow-man. For a moment George stood rooted to the spot. It had come so sudden. He could not move. A choking sensation came over him, and he could not speak.

Then he recovered himself, and as he bent over the dead young face he could not help saying, "Dear friend, was it for this we toiled and hoped and waited? Oh, what must death be in the world for, anyhow?"

As he turned away his glance fell upon an open Bible lying upon a little table near the head of the bed. He took the book up, and upon the page these were the words he read, underscored with heavy lines,—

"*Let not your heart be troubled; ye believe in God, believe also in me. In my Father's house are many mansions; if it were not so, I would have told you. I go to prepare a place for you. And if I go and prepare a place for you, I will come again and receive you unto myself; that where I am there ye may be also.*"

The words of our Saviour spoken to his disciples before he went away, what consolation they have brought to many a troubled heart!

The tears streamed from George's eyes as he read, and again turning over the leaves he came to this passage in the Book of Revelation, also heavily underlined,—

"*And I saw a new heaven, and a new earth; for the first heaven and the first earth were passed away; and there was no more sea. And I John saw the holy city, new Jerusalem, coming down from God out of heaven, prepared as a bride adorned for her husband. And I heard a great voice out of heaven, saying, Behold the tabernacle of God is with men, and he will dwell with them, and they shall be his people, and God himself shall be with them, and be their God. And God shall wipe away all tears from their eyes; and there shall be no more death, neither sorrow, nor crying, neither shall there be any more pain; for the former things are passed away.*"

He was about to close the book, but something inscribed on the cover within caught his glance, and there, wonders upon wonders, was the very poem he had written some time before, in the Indian boy's own handwriting, the closing words of which stood out more prominent than any of the others,—

> When mortal man has turned to clay;
> When proud and meek have gone their way;
> When weak and strong, and bond and free
> Are gathered down at death's dark sea;
> Then he whose faith's been greatest tried
> Shall gain the best and brightest side.

He laid the book down, astonished and bewildered, and as he did so he heard the very words uttered he had spoken on one occasion to Paul,—

"In human life men plan and build as though it were eternal, forgetting that death is in the world; and even as we build the silent reaper comes along and takes us away, and all that we have constructed soon passes into decay. How much better it is, then, to look beyond this life and build for that eternity which awaits us beyond the grave. Human life has its purpose, and the chief end of man is to glorify God. Just as we do this, then, and practise the heavenly virtues in mortal life, we shall be called to have a part in that higher, immortal existence, which knows no ending, where death and decay shall never enter."

He turned towards the Indian with whom he had entered the room, for it was he who had spoken, and as he looked upon him a mist swam before his eyes; then everything suddenly seemed in a whirl, and then he became aware that he was sitting in the office of the agency hotel. As he started up and looked around, the hotel-keeper entered the door, saying, "Well, woke up, have you? Went out a while ago and left you asleep in your chair. Hope you had a good rest. Supper is all ready; but your friends haven't got back yet. Guess they must have went from the school-house across the valley, to where Red Cloud lives. They'll probably be here soon."

George made no reply, but went to the door. The sun had sunk away and twilight was settling down upon the spot. A feeling of utter loneliness had taken possession of him, that became all the more intensified as he looked out upon the deserted street, the sombre buildings, and the desolate wastes of land that stretched away in every direction. Suddenly the ringing of the mission-bell broke the stillness, calling the members to evening worship. Led by some irresistible impulse, George started in the direction from whence the sound came, and in a few moments stood on the threshold of the little building. Service had begun as he entered, and he stepped quickly to one of the rear seats just as the whole assemblage bowed their heads in prayer. When he looked up again he gave a great start, for there, standing before the congregation with an open Bible in his hands, stood the one for whom he sought.

When the service was over that evening, another occurred where only two were met together in His name, that must have caused the hosts of heaven to rejoice.

"I see you have commenced your part of the proposition," said George, when the first greetings were over; "I have come to begin mine."

"May God bless and help us both!" was the reply.

And the agreement was further sealed by clasped hands.

APPENDIX.

THE following extracts are taken from a little treatise, entitled "The Future Indian," published by the author at the time of the Messiah craze among the Indian tribes of the West, in the fall and winter of 1890-91, and the attendant troubles with the Sioux at Pine Ridge and Standing Rock Agencies:

GLIMPSES OF THE BAD INDIAN.

. . . Let us glance for a moment at the "bad Indian." In the summer of 1886 I was living in Gordon, Nebraska, a settlement which sprung up on the Fremont, Elkhorn and Missouri Valley Railroad when that line pushed into the northwestern part of the State and the Black Hills. Owing to its close position to the Pine Ridge Indian Agency, the government established an Indian freight depot at that point, afterwards moving it to Rushville, an adjoining town. Gordon soon became a favorite lounging-place for many of the Indians, and seldom a day went by when some of them were not in town with their squaws and "pappooses." I never saw anything in these Indians of an inspiring nature. Excepting the freight-carriers, they did not represent a very industrious element. In fact, they were not of the progressive ones, who generally stay more at home and take care of their lands and ponies. They belonged to the bad Indian class,—the bad Indian as I saw him, for those were "weak, piping times of peace," and the ghost dance was not yet on to rouse the warrior spirit sleeping within him. Lazy, dissolute fellows, they would shroud themselves in a blanket on a hot day, and lean against the side of a building, and stand motionless as a statue for hours, and then, overcome by so laborious an undertaking, would amble off towards their tee-pees, and lie down on the prairie, to soon drop into a sweet, peaceful slumber. Meanwhile, the squaws would be running around doing all the work necessary.

Even the best of the Indians are disposed to shift all the hard work on the squaws, and the freight-carrier especially finds her a helpmeet, indeed, in his business. Once I saw a squaw coming up the street, bent almost to the ground, with a heavy wooden bedstead on her back, while her liege lord marched on in advance with all the dignity of a general whose duty it was to direct but not take active part in the campaign of work.

One day a band of Indians came over from the agency and gave an Omaha dance. It was a novel exhibition, and the people of the town raised a collection of nearly a hundred dollars for the performers. The Indians departed, happy as kings are supposed to be, but a week had hardly passed when they again put in an appearance, ready to give another performance, providing they should be as liberally rewarded as on the first occasion.

There was one old fellow, who cast his fortunes with the people of Gordon, named Thunder Hawk, an ex-warrior. He belonged properly at the Rosebud agency, where he was implicated in some way with the murder of Spotted Tail, and at his trial was banished from his own tribe and sent to Pine Ridge. An inveterate and shrewd gambler, he won from the Pine Ridge

Indians their ponies and blankets so completely that they arose in a body and drove him away from the reservation. So he came to Gordon, where he remained for a long time, haunting the saloons and gambling-resorts, and many a time fleecing some drummer or travelling man who mistook him for an innocent and endeavored to show him how to play pool and poker.

In the obtaining of rations, the bad Indian, it seems, manages to even up sometimes with the Indian agent for the deception and injustice which we are told that official is guilty of, and when a census is taken of the Indians it is not uncommon, I am informed, for many to loan their children to each other, and thus have their families rated much higher than they really are.

Well, perhaps the reader has been shown enough of the bad traits of the Indian. I allude to them here, because when we take up the Indian question we ought not to conceal anything. The best act we can do the Indians is to expose and condemn that which is subtle and deceptive in their nature, and point out and persuade them to abandon all that is lamentable, weak, and foolish. But in the work of reformation we should not judge the whole race by the bad Indian or the hopeless cases. As well might we apply the same principle to ourselves, where we have only to go down into the slums in our midst to find men sunk lower than the brutes,—men whose depravity would put to blush the meanest Indian that ever lived. We shudder at the atrocities which an Indian will commit, and yet every day we read in the newspapers of crimes by civilized man just as fiendish and brutal. The Indian, of course, should come out into the clear light of Knowledge and Wisdom, into that state unclouded by ignorance and superstition, into that manhood possessing moral responsibility and a desire for all that is high and noble; but it will be with him then, as it has always been with us, and he will fall and suffer, as we have fallen and suffered, whenever he accepts the Wrong in preference to the Right.

* * *

ANOTHER OUTBREAK.

Another "Indian outbreak," not unattended with destruction to human life, has occurred in the West,—this time among the Sioux. But, happily, through a wise and conservative policy, the troubles were brought speedily to an end, and a prolonged Indian war has been averted. During these troubles, charges of mismanagement and of injustice to the Indians came from sources that must be respected. Men do not usually go to war without some good reason. These Indians had some cause for their action, as has been clearly shown during the last four months. And now this question is before us: What are we going to do about it? Are there simply to be a series of receptions to the representatives of a people whom a month ago we denounced as treacherous vagabonds? Will we work ourselves into a furore, for the time being, over these delegates from Pine Ridge, and then forget all about them, after they have gone away? Are there to be a few more pledges made that, if adhered to at all, will be done so in a half-hearted way?

What was the lesson conveyed by this last Indian trouble?

This trouble differed from the previous ones, in that it possessed a religious aspect. It is significant that when despair comes to a man,—when he is completely lost, and all hope and earthly help is gone,—he will turn to some higher and immortal power to save him. So it was with the Indians. They did not know that that power had already come. True, missionaries had told them of a Messiah that had come to save all mankind, and some had believed. But many, in their simplicity, could not distinguish between the false and the true, and when civilization came and white men mistreated them and told them lies,—all lies,—they spurned the religion the white man brought, and wanted none of his civilization. They had never been offered our best civilization. The only real happiness they had ever known had been in the wild, free life of the past. They saw that could never be again. Their lands were gone, their game was gone, and the civilization they had learned to hate was every day creeping in upon them. In their despair they turned to an immortal power to save them. One day, one of their number who had been away in the Northwest came back and told them of a Messiah, whom he had seen and talked with, who was to take them all out of their troubles, who was to destroy the white people; and restore to the Indians not only their lands and abundant game, but their dead. No doubt there were some who took advantage of the craze that followed, and worked the Indians up to a frenzy that would bring on a war. But the most of them did believe the story and were sincere, and when actual warfare did come they faced death as only madmen would, firmly believing that the sacred robes they wore would shield their bodies from the soldiers' bullets. We all know the story of this whole affair. How the Indians inaugurated the strange ghost dance. How they practised it, until the white people became suspicious and alarmed. How an attempt was made to stop it, which only made the Indians more earnest than ever. How the soldiers then came, and how the Indians did not abandon the cause until their own blood had been shed and they began to realize the folly of it all.

The real Messiah, I have said, had come. That is what we believe. That is what we love to preach and sing about and read. We commemorate His birth in a beautiful manner every Christmas-time. Why, then, had He not come to the Indians as He had to us? Was it left for us to tell them about Him? If so, why have we not done it in a more general way?

* * *

INDIANS AS SOLDIERS.

"The supreme test of any scheme for benefiting humanity," wrote General Booth in "Darkest England," "lies in the answer to the question, What does it make of the individual? Does it quicken his conscience, does it soften his heart, does it enlighten his mind, does it, in short, make more of a true man of him, because only by such influences can he be enabled to lead a human life?"

General Booth had in mind the reclaiming of England's paupers and lost human beings when he wrote the above lines, but the question applies to all movements in behalf of humanity.

Several seemingly good reasons have been advanced for putting the Indians under military control, but I imagine the majority of those who favor this do so because they welcome a change of any kind that promises to take the Indians out of their present condition, and more so because a military man seems to understand the Indian's nature better than any other government official. But would it be the best policy? It is claimed that underneath military discipline the Indian could soon be trained into a good soldier, and thus become serviceable to the government, upon which he is now made a dependant. Somehow, it seems to me that—to speak in the vulgar parlance of the street gamin—"we're playin' it kind o' low" on the Indian when we do this. Supposing he does become a good soldier, and to some extent self-sustaining, would the conditions thus thrown around him tend to bring him up to the best type of manhood? I do not mean to belittle the soldier at all. We all love the soldier, the exemplar of honor and bravery, the man who will fight and give up his life in the discharge of duty. There are many good-hearted, clever men in the army, —able ones, too, who might attain prominence among citizens were it not for a strange fascination for military life. But what does the regular service really mean? So far as the privates are concerned, there is not one among them but will tell you, if he speaks out from the bottom of his heart, that it is a dog's life. Few men have entered it and not regretted the act afterwards. More than one capable fellow, to whom there happened to come some dark period,—one of failure and disappointment, and enforced idleness, likely enough,—has impulsively joined the regular army, and after three or four years of garrison and field life out West turns up at home some day, a rounded-off, subdued being in blue coat and brass buttons, shorn of the bright personality that once distinguished him. In the army men lose their individuality,—too often all ambition is crushed out of them,—the natural and only result where everything is strict discipline and duty. In the army, too, men become clannish, and maintain a cold, almost cynical, attitude towards the rest of the world. Out West the soldier has little love for the citizen; and as for the common settler, why, he is looked upon with contempt,—a "land-grub,"—a creature vastly inferior to the Indian.

Let us find something for the Indian better than the soldier's life.

What could have been more fatal to the real Indian cause than the brilliant military review held by General Miles, at Pine Ridge, recently? I suppose the main object was to impress upon the Indians the size and strength of the troops, although they had just learned the soldiers' power and the folly of attacking them. But imagine what the feelings of those savage warriors must have been when they looked down upon the spectacle from the bleak eminence upon which they had gathered. They saw only the outward show,—the dazzling display. To the most of them, especially the younger element, it was a glittering reality, and there could have been only one lasting effect produced,—a desire for such a life,—a mad passion to be a soldier.

A standing army in the West, while necessary for the restoring of peace in time of trouble and rebellion, has all along, in my opinion, retarded the Indians in their industrial progress. Its appearance upon any little scare or trouble has dismayed the conservative ones, while its uniform and glitter, its apparent life of ease, has aroused the admiration and envy of the others, and made them discontented in any other service. If we place the Indians under military control for the purpose of making some soldiers and some farmers, let us be careful that we do not check them entirely in their industrial advancement. For the best of them, the young and able-bodied, the bone and sinew of the nation, the very ones needed to carry on the home life, would be taken into the service, where, if they were dealt with equitably and paid as are the other soldiers, there would be no necessity for them at least to do any other work. If, however, the plan applies only to the bad element, the hostiles, and these are the ones to be converted into loyal soldiers, then the matter presents itself to me in this light: The principal reason for an army out West has been to keep this element in subjection. Make an army out of them, and nothing would remain for them to do, excepting the ordinary work which a certain number of well-trained police could attend to. Like the Dutch corporal in the late war, the hostile would be made a guard over himself,—made the victim of a huge joke. All that he would have to do would be to "spy his shadow in the sun," pose before the dusky maiden, and once in a while shoot down an imaginary foe.

Well, some reader here exclaims, this argument is growing ridiculous. It implies that an army is a needless, demoralizing thing, and the only reason for stationing one on the frontier is to keep peace among the Indians; any one ought to know that it would be folly to leave the frontier exposed and open to invasion; a standing army should be there at all times. But, dear reader, let me remind you that America is not divided into numerous governments,—like Europe, —aggressive, selfish, always scheming to enlarge their boundaries. The United States is not surrounded by powerful nations, ready at any time to invade and seize a portion of our domain; but is one mighty Republic, occupying nearly the whole inhabitable part of a great continent. England and Germany may need a standing army with which to conquer "Darkest Africa," and to retain their other vast possessions; Russia may need one in order to maintain the most despotic monarchy that ever existed; every little dynasty in Europe may need a standing army to keep its throne from toppling over; but peace-loving America, with an unselfish, friendly policy towards all nations, does not want a standing army.

Should there be danger of invasion, or of internal strife, we can soon meet it with a competent army. When the Southern Rebellion broke out, what a response there was to President Lincoln's call for troops? Everybody that could fight enlisted, and even the small boy wanted to go. All differences were forgotten. Old enemies became friends, and marched away, side by side, loving comrades. Down to the South went the people of the North, and in the war that followed they made a splendid fight. So did their enemy, some their own kindred. And when the war ended, with right triumphant, both forces, but with broken ranks where death had come, returned to their homes ready to take up the thread of civil life that had been so long broken.

Prudence, I suppose, would dictate that a United States army, such as we now have, should be maintained, but there is no necessity for increasing it in this, a time of peace, and in case of war we can call into use our National Service, increased and strengthened by our patriotic citizens, ever ready "to respond to their country's call."

I hope the time will come when men will no longer go to war. When armies will be a thing of the past. When every government will be for the people, by the people. When the world will be at peace. When there will be no uncivilized man. Such a day is no doubt far distant; but its coming is possible, and if we would make it so, surely we ought not to perpetuate among a savage race of people—whom we seek to uplift—institutions opposed thereto.

INDIANS AS CITIZENS.

It has been said that the land in the Sioux country and the adjoining region is not fit for agricultural purposes, and in proof of this some have stated that there are not as many people on the government land there to-day as there were ten years ago. I do not know that this is the case, but I should not be surprised if it were so in some sections. It was poverty, however, that drove the people away, if they have come away, and not because the land could not be tilled. With the exception of the sand-spotted districts,—there is, by the way, a desert ninety miles in length between Gordon and Valentine, Nebraska, a region of sand-hills,—some fine land lies out there, and particularly so in the Sioux reservation. Of course, in its primitive condition it may not look promising. Neither did the prairies of Illinois or Iowa forty years ago. The country has its setbacks and bad seasons. So do the best farming regions in the East. Cyclones and blizzards rage through the East now as well as the West. But of what use is land to a man without the means to till it? The people who settle upon our Western prairies do not as a general thing possess very much money. The majority go West for a home because they can find none in the East, and we never dream of the toil and hardship they undergo in the effort to secure it. The writer spent several months in an isolated region in Nebraska bordering the Sioux reservation. The nearest railroad point was Long Pine, forty-five miles away. The settlers' houses were made of sod, taken from the prairie, with earth for the floor, and willow poles covered with sod and dirt and straw for the roof,—a covering that let in a hundred little rivulets when a storm came along. In the winter, when the wind and storms drove down from the northwest, it was impossible to keep the snow from beating in. All the settlers had to live upon was the products of their claims. In most cases tea or coffee was a luxury, and wheat-bread was unknown until wheat could be raised and converted into flour, not a very easy thing in a country where grist-mills are miles and miles away. The land was rich and fertile, and the settlers raised acres and acres of corn and wheat. One could stand and look across the prairie and see nothing but fields of growing corn stretching away for miles. But there was no market for any of it that year, and the man was in luck who could sell a wagon-load of corn for a dollar. The only real benefit it gave the settler was when he used it for fuel that following winter. I have not exaggerated here in the least, but have given the reader a true picture of the Western claim-holder's life. Under such circumstances, is it any wonder that claims become abandoned, and the settling up of some regions is slow? The country I refer to was new, and the settlers needed money to build it up and connect it with the rest of the world. They had no money, and just starved along with the hope that capital would come in some day and give them a start. If they had had the money, they could have soon created one of the finest little farming districts in the West. High or low tariff, free trade or protection, the law of supply and demand, etc., etc., "had nothing to do with the case," as it stood then. They were starting a new enterprise, and they needed a little hard cash to begin operations with.

Now, why cannot the Indians, properly encouraged by not only the government, but all people as well,—Christians and philanthropists,— do what those settlers might have done?

Persuade the Indians to give up their fire-arms and discontinue their wild, repulsive dances. Gradually place them upon homesteads all over the reservation, with comfortable cabins to live in at first instead of the ragged teepee, and provide them with the means to cultivate the land. Change the trading-posts into industrial centres. When the Indian boy leaves the school let there be a workshop for him to enter, instead of loitering in the trading-store or skylarking over the reservation. Instead of buying the manufactured article at a large contract price, send the raw materials out and let the Indians be usefully employed and learn to supply their own demands. There is nothing impracticable about this. You have simply to put the shop and factory there, manned at first with competent white people, and commence with the graduates of the Indian schools,—bright, active young fellows that they are, many no doubt eager to undertake something of this kind. Or another plan suggests itself. When General Miles returned from Pine Ridge to Chicago, he brought with him the leaders in the Sioux outbreak, and stationed them at Fort

Sheridan, where an effort is now being made to train them into soldiers and to make of them future peace-makers among their people. It is also proposed to bring two hundred more East for the same purpose, as soon as possible. Now, suppose the object of this movement had been to make citizens of these Indians instead of soldiers. Suppose these Indians had been put through a preparatory training course, and then given every opportunity to become useful men.* Suppose these

---

* "Probably nothing has done so much to change the current of public opinion as to the possibility of civilizing Indians as the experiments in the education of Indian youth at the Carlisle and Hampton schools. The great work which these institutions have since accomplished grew out of the remarkable experiment made by Captain Pratt with a party of Indian prisoners who were confined by the government in the old Spanish fort at St. Augustine, Florida. These men, taken red-handed on the warpath, and imprisoned far from the scene of their crimes, as being especially dangerous outlaws, were so changed by Captain Pratt's judicious treatment, and by the efforts of a few Christian women for their instruction, that many of them became anxious to learn trades and to adopt habits of civilized life. In order that a fair opportunity might be

Indians could have come to learn the various trades and callings, to go back some day and help build up their nation. But let us take the Indian school graduates, and bring them East and apprentice them at the different trades, and we

---

given them to make this new departure, a few of their number were for a while taken to the Hampton negro training-school at Hampton, Virginia, and were there set to work along with negro boys. As these efforts promised success, the old government barracks at Carlisle, Pennsylvania, were fitted up as a training-school, and the work of Indian education was there definitely begun under the superintendency of Captain Pratt. The work for the negro at Hampton was also supplemented by the addition of two hundred Indian pupils. These two great schools, at which the Indian youth of both sexes and drawn from every tribe have been gathered, have been an object-lesson of the highest value to the Indian cause. Doing their work openly in the heart of Eastern civilization, they have shown our most intelligent people what they may be pardoned for not having believed before, that under favorable circumstances the Indian can be taught all that is necessary to fit him for at least an humble position in civilized life."—HERBERT WELSH, *Secretary Indian Rights Association, in New England Magazine.*

will soon have the material for our factory at the trading-centre.

What the Indians want, first of all, is more self-government than they now possess. Indians are not all ignorant, by any means. There are many sensible ones, who know better than any one else what is best for their people. The management of the Indians should be intrusted to a Governing Board—possessing some of the powers of a territorial legislature—composed of white officials commissioned by the government and Indians taken from the best and conservative element. Let a body of this sort take charge of the work that was sought to be done through Indian bureaus, commissions, and agencies, combining with it such a policy as is briefly outlined in the preceding lines, and the coming age may see the Sioux "reservation" changed to the Sioux commonwealth, its people neither savage wards nor savage soldiers, but citizens,—free men, happy and industrious. The Indians cannot be brought into this state of existence? Well, I don't know about that. Time works out some hard problems when men soften their hearts towards each other;

and it would be a grand privilege for any of us to help so lift up the Indian.

* * *

The Indian's Messiah has come. Not the one who was to roll back the earth upon the white people, and restore to the Indians their dead, their lands, and their game; but the Saviour of Mankind, the one who walked upon the earth long ago and taught a doctrine that was to bind all people—all races—into a fellowship of love and peace. The religion He taught—Christianity —was to give to the world a new life, a civilization grander than any the world had ever seen before. He commanded those who heard Him to go into every part of the world and reveal the Truth He spoke of, and to give the life He spoke of, to all who were in darkness. The inspiration this man brought into the world will ever remain, and to-day Christianity is the life, the soul, the purity, of civilization. As this Christian civilization spreads over the earth, and comes in contact with those who have never heard of the Christ, is it going to remember the divine command? Is it going to save? Is it going to impart the true life? If not, then, indeed, it would become an inconsistent, distorted thing,—a mocker of its own soul. Christianity has done much for the Indian, but not all that it might. True, we should not confound the false with the real, but there has been too much indifference, too much selfishness, on the part of a professed Christian people, too much injustice on the part of a Christian government. The wrongs of the past, however, may be atoned for in a measure by rendering justice in the future, and we can best show our love for the dead Indian, who has been injured, by caring for the ones who survive him. It is the Indian of the present and the future Indian with whom we have to deal.

The Sioux have been given more recognition than any other body of Indians (in return for the lands ceded by them); homes have been built for many of the people, and schools for their children, while an enormous amount of money is expended annually in providing them with food and clothing; but as a body of people, as human beings, they are not being rightly dealt with. Treaties have been made that were not kept entirely sacred, and promises have been made that are not yet fulfilled; but, worst of all, a system of management has been set up which makes an autocracy possible, beneath which many Indians lose all personal liberty and become more degraded than the Southern slaves ever were,—a condition entirely out of place in a country which believes that all men possess certain rights God has given them,—chief of which is happiness and manhood,—and that no man shall be deprived of those rights. Let us begin now to deal with the Sioux in a more consistent, honest manner. Tell them of the true Messiah, not as we have,—the Church sending out a few missionaries, and the State throwing around them obstacles that would dishearten the angels themselves. Give them your whole religion. Give them your civilization, with its inspiration for the sublime and noble. Give them your love, your sympathy, and your strength. Throw about them the influences that shape out the perfect human life,—that make the true man. Do this, and it will not be necessary to place them under "military control," or any other sort of "control," in order to solve the "vexatious Indian problem," for the problem will then find its only solution.

And what is best for the Sioux Indians is applicable to all the others.

THE END.

www.ingramcontent.com/pod-product-compliance
Lightning Source LLC
Chambersburg PA
CBHW032225230426
43666CB00033B/1531